THE KNOWLES FAMILY

A collection of historical research, memories & stories

William Albert Knowles
Jill Florence Maura Clowes (Nee Knowles)
Muriel Rooney Dell (Nee Couchman)
Edward Raymond Ian Knowles
Barry Matthew Knowles
Ivan Keith Knowles
Patrick Knowles

Published by WriterMotive
www.writermotive.com

Contents

Foreword

It was at a family gathering that William Albert Knowles was first inspired to research the Knowles family history. There was a discussion regarding Edward Knowles, William's great grandfather, born in 1836, and how he first came to Milton. Some of the family members seemed to think he was a tramp who had arrived on a barge to look for work; although William thought otherwise. This was the catalyst that started a 16 year research project that would see William not only prove that Edward was not a tramp, but that he was a descendant of a Knowles family that can be traced back to the 1500s in Kent, England, and pending additional sources, as far back as 1270.

It must be pointed out, that William's research in the 1980s and early 1990s was done before the internet existed in its current form, so his genealogy research meant travelling to parishes and churches as well as joining societies such as the Kent Family History Society and visiting Somerset House in London. It was harder and more time consuming back then, but perhaps more rewarding.

It was some years later that a post office customer of Jill Florence Maura Clowes (who happened to be the secretary of the Kent Family History Society) got talking to her about geneaology, this eventually lead to Jill making contact with William. Jill, the great granddaughter of Edward of Milton, was given the names of five people who also happened to be researching the name Knowles, one of them being William, with whom she shared the common ancestor, Edward.

In 2013, Edward Raymond Ian Knowles, the great great grandson of Edward of Milton, came into possession of a family tree, created by long deceased relative, Harry Thomas Rogers. This Family tree inspired Edward to dig further. He made contact with his second cousin Ivan Keith Knowles, also the great great grandson of Edward, and it was through Ivan (who had known Jill through his business 'Coinmatics') that he was put in touch directly with Jill. It was the beginning of a collaborative journey that has lead to this book.

In November 2014, Ivan hosted a gathering at his home in Whitstable, Kent. It was here that information, research and stories were exchanged. Subsequently, Jill had the idea of building on a family story written by William and also some family information written by the deceased Muriel Rooney Dell - granddaughter of Edward of Faversham - adding to their work and updating it to the modern day. It was then agreed to collate everything into a single book, that would serve for posterity for the future generations of the Knowles family.

Further contact was made with other Knowles, including Barry Knowles, great grandson of James Pankhurst Knowles who established a branch of the Knowles family fruit business in Dublin, Ireland. Barry joined the growing list of authors of this book along with Patrick Knowles, great grandson of Edward of Faversham.

Great care has been taken to accurately share information that if cannot be made certain by memory/first person account, then is backed up by mulitple sources. Modern day genealogists and other researchers all too often erroneously assume that any information found on the internet is always correct. We, as humans are the sources for that information.

While there are multiple sources and independent research made by several family members that can trace a direct line back to Thomas Knowles born in 1577, there is also further research online that claims we can continue to trace a line back to a William Thomas Knollys born in Hereford, England in 1270. At the time of writing, that would take a direct Knowles bloodline going back 747 years!

So why do we even have a surname? For thousands of years there was simply no need for a surname, people rarely travelled, they lived in small hamlets and villages, everybody knew their neighbour. According to the United Nations, in 500 AD the world population was as low as 190 million people, a figure that is dwarfed in comparison to the estimated 7.5 billion people that populate the world as of 2017. Times change, and as it did the population expanded, hamlets became villages, villages became towns. It also became increasingly useful to distinguish people when they were recorded in written records, particularly tax records. There simply needed to be a more efficient way of keeping track of people who shared the same first name.

Surnames had many different sources, but it is generally agreed that Western civilised countries developed names from one of four ways: patronymic, locative, occupational, and nicknames.

Patrynomic surnames. The majority of surnames are derived from the name of a male ancestor. These evolved from pre-existing non-permanent naming customs whereby an individual was identified by reference to a male ancestor or ancestors. Some example are: Bedo ap Batho ap Heylin (Welsh: Bedo, son of Batho, son of Heylin), which would become Bedo Batho; Lars Andersen (Scandianvian), Andrew MacDonald (Scottish: Andrew son of Donald) and Henry fil. Grimbald (English: Henry son of Grimbald). Such names are essentially the name of the father, sometimes with a suffix or prefix to denote the name as a patronym. For example, Armenian patronyms typically end in -

ian, Polish patronyms end in -ski and Irish patronyms begin with Fitz-.

Locative surnames can be derived from features of a landscape (Hill, Ford) or from place names (London, Aston, Eaton, Molyneux). Those surnames derived from place names were initially adopted by families that held land. However, later such adoptions of surnames derived from place names occurred when people moved from one place to another.

Occupational surnames derived from the occupation of an ancestor are also common, with Smith being the most common surname in the UK. This category of surnames is divided into two groups: standard occupations and titular occupations, such as Stewart, derived from an ancient clan title in Scotland.

Nickname surnames are less common, partly as they were often derived from unflattering characteristics such as: stupidity, girth, baldness and sometimes outright insults like Blackinthemouth. Many of these surnames have disappeared. There is on the other hand good survival of surnames derived from positive or neutral characteristics; Trow & Triggs (meaning trustworthy), Young, White and Good.

Of course, a family is more than just a surname, a family has a personality, its own set of core values and principles, a distinguishing identity and mentality that is passed down from generation to generation. Those are the things that truly define a family.

The stories inside this book are unfinished, and it is up to the future generations of the Knowles family to to help complete them... maybe it is you?

William Albert Knowles
1925 - 2001

Written in 1991

The earliest date that the Knowles family can definitely be traced is 1595 when Thomas Knowles married Elizabeth Knight at Gillingham. Their first child, a daughter, Frances was born there, but most of the others were born at Birling where the family stayed for over two hundred years.

Other Knowles's can be found at earlier dates in other parishes around Birling – Ightham, Snodland and Leybourne also in the Birling parish register William son of John Knowles was buried in 1568 and in the Assize record a Stephen Knowles a carpenter at Sevenoaks was hung with two others for sheep stealing in 1598. But these are only individual entries in the records and cannot be definitely connected with our family although they may well be. The only area that could be the source is Gravesend where there was a large Knowles family at the relevant period-the mid sixteenth century. If Thomas did come from Gravesend it might be possible to link up with a much earlier Knowles family, which I will go into further later on.

Registers were started at the Reformation in 1538, but in 1596 an order was made stating that the details must be copied into books of a stated quality, before then probably they were put in any book that came to hand. The order stated that all the records, at least from the start of the present reign should be copied into the new books; the reign of Elizabeth I began in 1558 that is why some Registers start then and some in 1538.

Many parishes have lost their earlier registers and their records do not start until much later, so the fact that a birth or marriage cannot be found in a certain area doesn't necessarily mean that a family was not in that area. Before 1538 it is very difficult to trace a family, sometimes a will can be found, but not all wills have survived and an individual had to have a certain amount of wealth to make a will.

Thomas was mentioned twice in the Quarter Sessions, in 1605 he was bound over to keep the peace concerning William Huggyn of West Mailing and in 1609 he stood surety for someone in Birling. He was described in the Quarter Sessions as a Husbandman, in the true sense a Husbandman is anybody concerned in working on the land, but by this time it had become the status of someone between a labourer and a yeoman, usually it was a person who rented a few acres and at harvest time or at other seasons would hire his labour out. They usually regarded themselves as of equal status to yeomen and in some of the inventories of their property compiled when they died they lived in better style than 'yeomen'.

In 1605 Thomas was one of a group of Birling residents who sent a letter to the Justices concerning a Jane Jacket or Jean Jacquette, she was hired by the parish of Ryarsh to nurse her family who had the plague; after all the family had died she was driven from Ryarsh and became a vagrant. She became pregnant and returned to Ryarsh but when the time of the birth came the residents of Ryarsh drove her out of the parish into Birling and stood watch to make sure she stayed there because the child of a vagrant became a charge on the parish in which it was born. Later in 1609 at Rochester Assizes she was charged with stealing from a number of people in Birling, including Thomas

Knowles. She was found guilty of larceny and remanded on a plea of pregnancy. At this period a theft of any property worth more than twelve pence was classed as Grand Larceny and punishable by hanging. At this time the ancient law of Benefit of Clergy still held good which meant that if you could read and write, no matter how badly, you were let off. This was a legacy from the middle ages when the only people who were literate were the clergy who were tried in their own special courts and not in the Assizes which had no power to prosecute them. This was main bone of contention between Henry II and Becket back in the twelfth century, I believe the law was abolished some time in the reign of James I.

Thomas's first wife died in 1613 and he married Susan who died in 1622, her surname and where he married I haven't traced.

In his will dated l0th, July 1623 he left his bedstead and furniture and twenty five pounds to his daughter Frances and his pewter to be divided equally between her and his other daughter Ethelinda. The rest of his goods he divided between his sons. His inventory, the list of moveable objects such as furniture, farm stock and farm implements hasn't survived; this was compiled for Death Duties, only moveable goods were listed, land and property were not taxed. Some inventories were very comprehensive even listing chamber pots and dog collars, it all depended on who made the list, sometimes they were done by neighbours and were very short.

Not much is known of his sons, we are descended from Richard, William died in 1646 and left land and property in Birling.

William's sons were much wealthier, one of them, another Richard had several farms in Birling and the surrounding villages including Coney Hatch and Park Barn in Birling and Castle Farm at Leybourne, which still exists. In his inventory Richard had moveable goods totalling £1659, his brother Williams inventory amounted to £1716 and at today's values they would probably be approaching millionaires, William in his inventory owned or rented Birling Place the ancestral home of the Nevilles in Kent, a Neville lives there now, but in 1692 the date of the inventory it had degenerated into a farmhouse, very poorly furnished and probably occupied by a tenant.

Richard and his brother Henry were among those who paid for a clock and dial to be put in the tower of Birling church in 1699. The present clock dates from the late 1800s and was put there by the Marquis of Abergavenny whose Neville ancestors are buried there.

Henry and his son John were very likely the owners of Hurst in Otterden mentioned by Hasted. They probably never lived there as I can't find them in the Otterden register.

Other Knowles's living in Birling one was John who married Jane the widow of Archibald Crampton who it is believed lived at Birling Place. In the register they are always referred to as Mr.John and Mrs.Jane Knowles this is very unusual, the only other instance I know of is Richard Knowles at Sandwich who was always referred to as Mr., I think it is meant to be a sign of status.

In a book based on the diaries of the Hayes family who lived at Howletts (A Yeoman of Kent by R.Arnold), a Richard Hayes who lived 1692-1754 said that he bought his cherry sieves from Mr.Knowles of Trosley for eight shillings a dozen. This would probably be Nicholas or one his sons who lived at Trosley at this time. Sieves were wicker baskets of various measures that were used for sending fruit to market up until about the second war. The last ones I used were in 1950 when the salesman ran short of wooden boxes.

Our ancestor William was born in Birling in 1692-93, he farmed at Ryarsh, Ditton and Boughton Aluph, dying at B.Aluph in 1731, I have his inventory which totalled £710 but does not give the name of the farm which according to the inventory was quite large, his will has not survived and I haven't been able to trace the farm at B.Aluph. William had four children, three were born at Birling and John our ancestor was born at B.Aluph. William the elder son married a farmer's daughter at Plaxtol and founded a large family there, as the will is lost I don't know how the property was divided but I think William as the eldest inherited most of it.

John was born in B.Aluph in 1724 and married Mary Atwood there in 1746-47.

It was at this point that I became stuck it was only guesswork based on the similarity of the christian names that led me to think that we were descended from the Knowles family at Birling. I had traced our family from the present back to William at Tunstall who by age at death was born about 1750 who was probably a brother of John buried at St.Michael's Sittingbourne who was also born in the 1750s. It took several years searching records to find where John from B.Aluph settled and if William and John were his sons. Eventually I found the answer in the Bishop's Transcripts at the Cathedral Library Canterbury. John went from B.Aluph to Lynsted and raised all his family there, what his trade was and if he was left any property by his father I haven't found out. His eldest son William died aged sixteen months, only nine days later he christened another baby William. This continuous use of same names, William, Richard, Thomas and John may be of use in tracing the family back much further than can traced in the registers.

This second William was our ancestor, he was born in 1755 and his brother John was born in 1757. John later went to Sittingbourne where he married Elizabeth Gambier, Gambier is a Huguenot name, her family probably came from Canterbury where the Huguenots first settled. John started a firm of plumbers painters and glasiers in Sittingbourne which continued at least until 1891 when they had premises at 113 High Street. They were also engineers to the local fire brigade at least one of them serving with it.

William married Elizabeth Smead at Sittingbourne in 1776 his eldest son John was our ancestor, he was baptised at Sittingbourne in 1777, I believe it was the custom for the first born to be baptised in their mothers, parish. Most of Williams' children were born at Tunstall apart from one who was born at Borden, and Mary the youngest who I have been unable to trace where she was born. William died at Tunstall in 1831, there is no evidence as to what he did but he may possibly have been a farm bailiff, the house where he lived and where another son William lived after his death still exists-one of a row of cottages on the right hand side of the road before you reach Tunstall from Sittingbourne (Grid Ref.899619). The rent given in the Tithe Returns of 1841 is 2s.6d.

John our ancestor married Ethelinda Hull at Milton in 1798 and continued to live there. In 1814 when the fathers occupation is included in the Registers John is given as a gardener (market gardener) but in Pigotts' Trade Directory for 1824 and 1829 he is named as the licensee of the Watermans' Tavern in Milton, perhaps he retired as a market gardener, he is not in the 1841 Directory. John died in 1853 aged 75, he had thirteen children of whom three died as children, his third child and eldest son was Edward who was our ancestor, he was born in 1802, when his first child was baptised in 1826 he was described as a gardener as his father was. Also like his father he became a publican because in 1836 in the Register he gave his occupation as a victualler, in the Tithe Allotment about 1840 he occupies the Shipwrights Arms on Milton quay. In the 1841 Census he is a gardener again, living at Pound Row, Pound Row was once Hog Pound Row, obviously a select neighbourhood.

The child who was baptised in 1836 was Edward my great grandfather who was really the reason I started investigating our family because nobody seemed to know where he came from. At a family party when I said that I was trying to trace the family back and the problem was that Edward was born before the Census started some of the family said that he arrived in Milton as a tramp others said he arrived on a barge. At this time the registers were kept at the church of their origin, but later they were put in the County Record Office and were more easily available to the public and I was able to start on the family tree.

The family of William who married at Plaxtol seem to have lived there until quite recently, two Knowles's are on the 1914-1918 war memorial. William and his family owned or rented many farms in the Plaxtol area including the manor house of Old Soar, where they are recorded on the plaque there. A large tombstone in the floor of Plaxtol church lists William's family, four of his children died during August 1771, possibly of typhoid or diphtheria at that time of year.

Another William, according to his estate map dated 1825, owned all of the of the hamlet of Basted but in 1841 in the census he is recorded as a farm labourer. The cause is probably that the Napoleonic wars lasted nearly a generation and farmers became used to high wheat prices and a high standard of living and began to regard themselves as gentry. The Corn Laws kept wheat prices high after the war finished by imposing tariffs on foreign wheat, for the landowners of the Tory party this meant they could keep the farm rents high whereas the Whigs as the factory owners wanted cheap food so that they could pay low wages.

The farmers who couldn't adjust their style of living when the Corn Laws were repealed went bankrupt and many farms cut their labour force causing unrest among the farm workers and leading to the Courtney uprising at Dunkirk. Abband or bands calling themselves 'Captain Swing' terrorised the Kentish countryside burning ricks and barns and smashing the machinery that was brought in to replace the work force. A rhyme that survives from this time describes the process from self-sufficiency to gentrification to appearance as a bankrupt in the London Gazette.

1743	**1843**
Man, to the plough.	*Man, Tally-ho.*
Wife, to the cow.	*Wife, silk and satin.*
Girl, to the yarn.	*Girl, piano.*
Boy, to the barn.	*Boy, greek and latin.*
And your rent will be netted.	*And you'll all be gazetted.*

Williams house 'Cherry Banks' is still at Basted.

Edward of Milton was born in 1836, he baptised his first children in 1859, they were twins both died within a year; his occupation then was a baker, later he had a grocery and greengrocery in Milton High Street, these were combined with the Post Office as he was also the Post Master. In his spare time he was the School Board Attendance Officer and Town Crier. He was said to be a drunkard and was reputed to have reformed when he came home one night and heard one of his children praying for him... maybe. As usual when he stopped he believed everyone should stop and became a temperance reformer lecturing about the 'demon drink'. His nickname in Milton was 'Nibble', whether it referred to his eating habits or his morals I don't know.

He bought cherries on the trees at the annual cherry sale as all my family have done since and perhaps also did before him. My grandfather used to say how boring it was walking around the orchard all day, when he was a boy, bird-scaring with a rattle. He had several sons who were all in the fruit trade, the eldest surviving son was Horace Sparkes who continued at the Post Office, James Pankhurst and Charles both went to Aberdeen and started a shop, James later went to Dublin to open a shop. The Aberdeen shop is now quite large and still trades as Knowles and Son but no longer belongs to the family.

My father told me that Edward of Milton used to send William pears up to Aberdeen on a barge, of course when they reached there they were sleepy and soft, but they sent him a cheque to keep him happy. My father also said that when they first went to Aberdeen they needed backing, but when the business flourished they cut Edward out. Charles made a great deal of money, mainly on the Stock Exchange, he used to come back to Sittingbourne in a chauffeur driven Rolls.

Horace Sparkes, known as 'Sparko' kept the Post Office at Milton, he also bought fruit and had an orchard at Iwade. He is reputed to have had three wives and to run off with somebody else's. His son Douglas kept the post office after him.

Edward, another son started a fruit shop in Faversham, apparently he was well liked there and was once almost persuaded to stand as M.P. for Faversham, then he found out a deposit was required and pleaded ill health. He was reputed to have had a son by a woman in London and to have brought him back to Faversham and raised him as one of the family, I believe he was named Allen. Fairly recently when I was on holiday I met someone who said her father's name was Knowles and was a greengrocer who was born in Faversham and had broken with his family, his name was John Henry Attree Knowles, so I wonder if Edward brought more than one home?

William was another son and was my grandfather, he had a row with his father and started on his own with a horse and cart he bought with a loan from his father-in-law, Abraham Akhurst, who was a barge captain so my grandfather used the Red Anchor as a trade mark. The Akhurst family were barge captains as far back as I can trace. William had two shops in Sittingbourne, 20 High Street known as the top shop and 65 High Street called the bottom shop as well as one at 87-89 High Street, Sheerness and a wholesale round. The latter part of his life he lived in a fairly large house called Charlton House on top of Snipes Hill. On William's death his son Stanley lived there until 1988 when it was sold.

Edward married twice his, second wife was the sister of his first, at the time this was illegal so he had to marry in Jersey. He died in 1917. He died fairly well off, he lived in Milton in a house named 'Blenheim'.

When I started to try to trace the family back before the records started I was struck how much we resembled a family at the time of Elizabeth I. All the Roberts in both families died very young. I had an uncle and four cousins named Robert who died. The uncle died of pneumonia at about eighteen months and I suppose his brothers and sisters joined his name with that of their own children as a form of remembrance, but two died in childhood and two were killed in the second war. The only other Robert I found also died young aged 24 in 1664.

I will give the details of Elizabethan family later on, the most famous of the family was Robert Deveraux, Earl of Essex whose mother was Letitia Knollys.

The Knollys family claimed descent from Sir Robert Knolles, the mercenary captain in the Hundred Years War and used his coat of arms, but legitimately the furthest they could trace back was to Thomas Knolles a merchant who was twice Lord Mayor of London (1399 and 1410), although actually the Lord part of the title didn't start until a few years later. In his will the elder son Thomas inherited the business and the Manor at North Mimms in Hertfordshire and the younger son William was left 100 Marks (£66 13s.4d.). The succession of names Thomas and William began to lead me to wonder if it was possible that we were connected. The earliest William was in Birling in 1568 and from 1600 until the present day there has been a William in every generation and Thomas has been nearly as frequent.

I got the will of Sir Robert Knolles to see if I could trace any connection between the two families. The will was dated 1407 when he died at Sculthorpe in Norfolk, written half in Latin for the official business the personal bequests are in Norman-French. He appoints among others Thomas Knolles as one his executors so there must be some close connection between the two families.

Little is known of Robert Knolles, the historians agree that he came from Cheshire and that he was probably related to Sir Hugh Calveley and most state that he rose from a common soldier. He was probably born at Malpas in the 1320s, in his will dated 1407, he leaves a hundred ?? to the parish church - (*Item iea devise al esglise perochiell de Malpas de deinz la comite de Chestur pur nons and en memorie C*).

Malpas is a small hill town situated not far from the Welsh border, its original Saxon name was Deepdene, Malpas was the name the Norman holder gave to his castle - 'Evil Passage'. The castle was built on a Roman site as it lies on the Roman road from Wroxeter to Chester, it must have been the site of many skirmishes because one medieval source states that the English dead had to buried in the fields where they fell as the Welsh held Malpas church'. On the original Victorian Ordnance Survey maps a few miles east of Malpas is the place name 'The Knowles', possibly the source of the family name. Another local place name is 'No Mans Land', showing how disputed the area was. In the wills of the Calvelely family it seems that Robert was accepted as one of the family, in the will of Mabel de Calveley Robert Knolles is included with Hugh and David de Calveley. Mabel was the second wife of Richard de Calveley so it is likely that Robert was her son from a previous marriage. It is generally accepted that a cousin of Robert was a Hugh de Brow, the coats of arms of the two families are very similar, and Hugh de Brow is named as a executor in Robert Knolles will so it is possible that Roberts mother was Mabel de Brow and he was step-brother to Hugh de Calveley. And also Richard has been a name family ever since.

Robert married Constance de Beverley a member of a Yorkshire family, no children are mentioned in the will and as Robert was apparently an only child any descendants must be illegitimate. His first recorded military service was in Brittany in 1346 with Hugh de Calveley under Sir Thomas Dagworth at the siege of La Roche D'Orient. His birth date is unknown but about 1327 would be roughly accurate. It is fairly certain that he was knighted before 1351. The campaign in Brittany was between two factions both claiming the vacant Dukedom of Brittany, when the Duke, John, died his chosen heir was his niece who was married to the Charles de Blois nephew of the King of

France. A nephew, John de Montfort, son of another of the dead Dukes brothers disputed the claim and seized many towns and castles. Realising that the king would support Charles de Blois, De Montfort went to Edward III and paid homage to him as Duke of Brittany saying that he recognised Edward as the true King of France. Edward financed an expeditionary force to help John de Montfort gain Brittany. It was during a brief truce in the fighting that occurred what was called at the time 'chivalries finest military expression', monuments celebrate it in France although it is almost unknown in England, probably because we lost. Two castles in Brittany Joscelin and Ploermal were held by the opposing forces, Joscelin for Charles de Blois by Robert de Beaumanoir and Ploermel for de Montfort by Sir Bramborough. Both forces were professional soldiers and were probably bored, the castles were only ten miles apart and de Beaumanoir rode over and challenged Bramborough to single combat; this appealed to all of them so thirty of the best fighters from each side were chosen, it has been known since then as "The Combat of the Thirty". This wasn't to be a gentlemanly tournament on horseback with lances it was a fight to the death on foot with whatever weapon you fancied.

Robert Knolles and Hugh Calveley were both included in the English thirty, in the final stages of the battle just nine of the English thirty were left standing and were holding off the French survivors when one of the French left the field retrieved his horse and charged the English group, in the end Bramborough and eight of his team were killed and rest taken prisoner, all the survivors of both sides were wounded. Froissart says that twenty years later a French survivor at the French King's table was 'honoured above all'. An obelisk marks the spot between the two castles where the battle was fought.

In 1352 Robert Knolles was lieutenant to Sir William Bentley, who was Keeper of Brittany, when they encountered a force of French under Guy II de Nesle, the Marshall of France, the French version of the battle is that they were ambushed by an equal force, the English version is that they were a minute force trying to get reinforced from England. Bentley took position on a hill near Mouron when the French attacked, Bentley was wounded and the archers on the right were forced back, the archers on the left held and the men at arms fell back up the hill to a belt of trees and the French were halted and the archers routed them. Sir Robert Knolles had taken command and had thirty archers hung for retreating without orders. Six hundred French knights and nobles were killed or captured. So thick were the French dead that the body of de Nesle was not found for two days.

This battle was probably the foundation of Knolles' later immense fortune, if a prisoner could raise a ransom the man who took him would have two thirds, the other third going to the commander who in his turn would pay a third of that to the King. The King would sometimes buy the ransoms from a knight getting a discount for ready cash as it often took years for the prisoner to sell the land to raise the ransom. It was considered an insult if too low a ransom was set on you. Edward III paid Sir Thomas Cheyne £1483.6.8 for Duguesclin in 1367.

During periods of truce in the Hundred Years War bands of discharged soldiers would roam France sacking villages and holding merchants and travellers, the most desperate and feared of these bands was led by Sir Robert Knolles and Sir Hugh Calveley, known as The Great Company it is said that at one time they held more French castles than the French King. They held their own markets and employed their own lawyers and generally terrorised northern France. Any village or town that refused to pay them protection money was destroyed, a burnt house with its gable ends standing was known as a Knolles's Mitre. They also broke a number of English laws regarding prisoners and piracy which Edward III tolerated because it suited him to have a ready made army of professionals he could call up when the truces ended, saving the expense of a standing army. This worked well until in 1370 when Edward launched a raid through northern France, the French by this time has realised that it was useless opposing the English in battle where they were massacred by the archers and began a scorched earth campaign locking themselves in the walled towns and destroying the surrounding crops so that the English columns could not live off the land while they besieged the town, but were forced to move on in search of food then the French would harry and cut off the foraging parties. War began to lose some of its glamour and profit for the English troops, there were no more ransoms and easy victories just skirmishes and hunger and it became increasingly difficult to find volunteers. In preparation for his raid or as it was called a Chevauchee, Edward began trying to raise an army, his commanders were set to find by any means men to serve them, they were rewarded by leases of manors owned by the King.

Sir Robert Knolles was unable to raise the full number of men, although he cleared the gaols of prisoners who were granted pardons for service in France. A list of the prisoners shows that the bulk of them were murderers, so much for the yeomen of England. Landing at Calais his policy was to do as much damage as possible and support himself by plunder, to tie down the French forces to stop them reinforcing Aquitaine and if possible force a set piece battle; but although he sacked the suburbs of Arras and paraded in front of Rheims and was so close to Paris that the smoke of burning villages was visible there Charles V would not allow his army to fight. In September Knolles headed towards Normandy but was hindered by the younger knights in his party who were disaffected by the lack of ransoms and the glory of a pitched battle and led by Sir John de Menstreworth and one named Grandson, who said it was a slight that they should be led by a man they considered to be an adventurer, de Menstreworth and Grandson calling Knolles *'an old brigand'*. A large portion of the army broke away under their leadership and Knolles withdrew towards Brittany through Chartres and Chateaudun and spent November subduing various places in the Loire valley.

Du Guesclin was summoned from Aquitaine and went in pursuit, Knolles in the Brittany marches prepared to give battle and called Sir Hugh Calveley from St.Maur-sur-Loire. Ordered to rejoin him Grandson was on his way when he was caught by Du Guesclin at Pont Villain and totally defeated. Further action was now useless and the English forces withdrew to neighbouring fortresses and Knolles to his castle at Derval Although the expedition ended badly the recall of Du Guesclin relieved the pressure on Aquitaine Menstreworth on his return to England blamed Knolles for the failure and he was forced to send two squires to England to represent his case. Although he was cleared and Menstreworth was forced to flea to France the seven manors he had been given were withdrawn because he had failed to raise his quota of men. It was now that his other misdemeanours were raised, a list that included almost every crime in the book, to get a general pardon cost him ten thousand marks (6,666 pounds) probably several million pounds in today's currency before he could return to England.

In 1374 he was back in favour and was sent with an expedition to Aquitaine and placed in command of the fortress of Brest. He was with the Duke of Lancaster at the siege of St.Malo and with his cousin Sir Hugh Brow plundered the surrounding countryside. His last campaign in France was in 1380 under John of Gaunt through the same route from Calais to Brittany with much the same result but when they arrived in Brittany they found that John de Montfort, who they had always supported, was making peace with the new King of France Charles VI, Charles V having died.

Sir Robert Knolles' main manor in England was at Sculthorpe in Norfolk but when in London he stayed at his town house in Seething Lane near the Tower of London. He was there in 1381 when Wat Tyler led the Peasant's Revolt into London. Knolles, in full armour, led his armed retainers to the Tower to consult with the King now the very young Richard II, Edward III having died in 1379. His advice to the King was to 'give them the cold steel', but the King decided to talk to the mob and when Wat Tyler was killed by the Mayor of London told them 'let me be your leader' and got them to disperse. But afterwards he let Knolles loose on them and the King's law officers later searching their villages.

Richard's court was very luxurious and with his young Queen, Richard indulged in all the fashions and clothes. Silks and velvets all having to be imported, their cost was enormous, consequently Richard was always in debt and forced to seek loans. In the state records the 'Calendar of Patent Rolls' in 1382 Knolles was given plate and jewels from the Royal Treasury as security for loans totalling £6888 l0s 8d, the King saying about Knolles that he had, 'ever found him courteous and well disposed in the time of his need'. His wife, Constance, died in 1389, Knolles went on a pilgrimage to Rome, in the License giving him permission, the reasons for the pilgrimage were 'for the quieting of his conscience and the salvation of his soul in fulfilment of his vow'. He took twelve servants with him so he did not suffer much hardship. In 1991 I probably followed his route from Pisa to Rome; with Hugh Calveley and John Hawkwood another mercenary he is reputed to have founded a hospital for English pilgrims, but I haven't been able to confirm this.

He had many connections in this area, he was a trustee in the will of Sir Walter Manny another professional who came from Brabant with Queen Phillipa, the wife of Edward III. One of the properties in the will was on Elmley in Sheppey, another was Tunstall Manor later called Cromer's which Knolles bought in 1402. The Cromer family bought the manor soon afterwards, one Cromer was Lord Mayor of London and was beheaded in 1450 during the Jack Cade rebellion.

With Sir John Cobham he began the construction of a bridge at Rochester to replace the existing one, which was of wood and in a ruinous state; his new stone bridge lasted nearly five hundred years only being replaced late in the nineteenth century. His coat of arms and those of Cobham are the end of the bridge that replaced it, which was itself partially superseded by the M2 bridge further upstream of the Medway.

When the Great Cloister in Canterbury Cathedral was planned contributions for its cost were given by many of the nobility and any one giving over a certain amount would have a shield bearing his arms attached on display in the roof, today it is reputed to be the finest existing collection of medieval examples of heraldry in the world, there are three shields bearing Knolles' arms on display, the new rich were the same even then.

Another local connection is at Bodiam Castle in Sussex, this was built in 1385 by Sir Edward Dalyngrigge or Dalling Ridge, a place name near East Grinstead, who served under Knolles in France. The castle was built as a defence to stop the French sailing up the River Rother. So much did the French fear Robert Knolles that above the Postern

Gate, that faced south and would be the first thing anyone approaching from the river would see, he carved the arms and crest of Robert Knolles which are still there. In those days when only the clergy were literate the arms of a family were as good as a signature and would be known and recognised probably by most ranks of fighting men especially in battle when the instant recognition of them would tell you on whose side they were.

It is probable that the name Knolles was pronounced sounding the K, Barbara Tuchman, who wrote 'A Distant Mirror, The Calamitous Fourteenth Century', says that when she was researching the book it was in some documents spelt Canolles, she at first was under the impression she was dealing with two different people. This pronunciation stills exists, for instance in Canute and in Cannock Chase. The origin of the name is the Old English 'Cnol' meaning a small rounded hill.

Knolles died at Sculthorpe in 1407 and was buried next to his wife in the Carmelite Monastery at Whitefriars in London, this was dissolved by Henry VIII in 1538 and its ruins became a refuge and hiding place for criminals and outlaws, it was known as Alsatia and became notorious in later times. The area was finally cleared after it was devastated in the Great Fire of London in 1666. Fleet Street was built over the site, which is still called Whitefriars, the Daily Mail building when it was in Fleet Street was called Carmelite House. Knolles left large sums of money for prayers to be said for the souls of his wife and himself in perpetuity and to many other charities. He founded the Knolles Alms House in Pontefract the town where his wife was born and left them the bulk of his fortune and his clothes, as described in his will they must have been worth a fortune - one was of red silk powdered with gold. All his followers were named in his will and left money. He must have been at least eighty when he died.

Hugh Calveley died in 1393 his great tomb is in the chancel that he built in his home church at Bunbury in Cheshire, the village of Calveley from which he took his name is a few miles away, he had no known descendants.

As I have said Sir Robert Knolles named no heirs in his will but Thomas Knolles called a citizen of London was amongst the executors named and as Robert Knolles had no other family that is known, it is possible that he was an illegitimate son or perhaps grandson. In 1415 a Robert Knolles citizen of London was mentioned in another will, he could possibly be a brother of Thomas. Thomas was prosperous merchant in the Grocer's guild and was Mayor of London in 1399 and 1410, about the same time as Dick Whittington, they weren't called Lord Mayors until a little later. He owned a lot of property in London, but built his manor at North Mimms in Hertfordshire and also rebuilt most of the church. He had three daughters to whom he left each a gold ring worth 100 shillings, they probably also had their dowry. His elder son Thomas inherited all the property and the business, William the younger son was left 100 Marks, the Mark was not actually a coin but was used in transactions much as the Guinea is used at present, it was worth two thirds of a pound. It is from William that we are possibly descended; the elder son Thomas himself had two sons, it is significant that his eldest son was named Robert the younger son was named Richard.

The names Thomas, William and Richard have continued in our family in generation after generation with the name Robert always ill-fated just as it was in what is possibly the senior branch of the family.

After the death of Thomas Jr., who was buried in the church of North Mimms, his tomb has not survived neither has his will, the eldest son Robert lived in the manor at North Mimms. He married Elizabeth the widow of Sir

Hugh Venables who held land in Cheshire, she appears to have held land in Cheshire in her own right and to have bought the title to the marriage.

Robert appears to have become a prosperous landowner, and as a squire and minor gentry, which in this disturbed time brought with it uncertainty which faction to support. The Wars of the Roses began in 1455 and the crown and power had switched from one side to the other; in 1459 Robert was ordered to muster with the Hertfordshire Array by Henry VI then in 1461, the crown having switched to Edward IV, he was made one of the Commissioners in Hertfordshire to raise the fleet in Suffolk against Henry VI. In 1469 Edward IV held Henry VI captive in the Tower, Henry's queen Margaret was in exile in France, she was always the backbone of the Lancastrian party and was continually plotting and making alliances to oust the Yorkist party of Edward.

In 1469 a servant of Thomas Whittingham, one of the exiles with Queen Margaret in France, named Cornelius was caught smuggling letters from Whittingham to Thomas Danvers in England, when he was questioned and tortured in the Tower he named many Lancastrian supporters among the squires was Robert Knolles, what happened is unknown but on his tomb at North Mimms, no date of death is given for him, which suggests that the tomb was built when his wife died and the brasses inscribed with both their names but no one knew the fate of Robert. At this period in the Wars most of the leading families on both sides had at least two generations of heads of families either killed in battle or executed after being defeated. The main Lancastrians such as Owen Tudor, who was executed after the battle of Mortimer's Cross and the Beaufort family who were executed after the battle of Tewkesbury when Edward IV dragged them out them out of Tewkesbury Abbey where they had sought sanctuary after the battle.

Henry VI only son, also Edward, was killed in the battle and shortly after Henry VI was murdered in the Tower of London where he had been held prisoner for several years. The Yorkist families also suffered many losses, after the battle of Wakefield Edward IV's father, brother and uncle were executed and the head's of his father and uncle put over the gates of York. Edward IV even had his own brother, George Duke of Clarence, put to death for persistent treachery; so it can be seen that it didn't pay to hang around if you did become under suspicion. It was usually the die-hard families that suffered the worst such as the Cliffords the Nevilles and the Beauforts, it was recognised that minor gentry were only following their overlord and they usually only suffered loss of their land which could be restored to them or their heirs when things cooled down, but it probably didn't pay to take any chances. Robert only had two daughters who were his co-heirs so that his lands and property left the Knolles family when they married.

This left Richard the younger son to carry on as a merchant, in 1452 he seems to be concerned with the parish of St.Antony in London and in 1455 and 58 he is a commissioner of the Peace in Hertfordshire, also in the 1450s Thomas and John appear in the records they were probably Richard's sons. Thomas was in the Draper's Guild and John was in the Haberdashers and in 1470 was in the Array of the Earl of Essex. In 1470 a Robert, who is generally accepted as being Richard's grandson, appears, with others he seems to be concerned with the Abbot of St.Albans and was granted an annuity of twenty Marks by Henry VII.

With the deaths of Henry VI and his son the only surviving Lancastrian pretender to the throne was Henry Tudor, later Henry VII, his claim was tenuous, his father was the outcome of an illicit marriage between Owen Tudor and the widow of Henry V and his mother was Margaret Beaufort who was a descendant of John of Gaunt and his mistress.

In spite of this Edward IV regarded him as the last threat to his throne and made several attempts to either capture him or have him killed.

Henry Tudor eventually came to the throne by right of conquest in 1485; in 1488 in the State Rolls *"Grant for life to the King's servant Thomas Knolles, yeoman of the King's Own Mouth in the King's pantry. For services beyond the seas and in England the office of the keeping of the park of Mersshwood Dorset"* . This probably means he was the King's food taster, not exactly a job with long term prospects. For services beyond the seas probably means that he served Henry when he was in exile and was very likely present at the battle of Bosworth. The job of Keeper of the Park was a sinecure that had a salary but no duties, it had previously been held by Cicely, Duchess of York the mother of Edward IV and Richard III.

It seems that this branch of the Knowles family had finally backed the winning side in the Wars of the Roses and the rewards of so doing set them the on the path to preferment that has lasted to the present day. In 1488 Robert was appointed to wait on 'the King's dearest son', Arthur, and was rewarded with £5 for each of the three years (1488-90) and when in 1490 he accompanied the King as one of the Usher's of the Chamber he continued in the same office under Henry VIII. In 1514 he was granted the manor of Rotherfield Greys near Henley at an annual rental of one red rose on midsummers day, this strangely, or significantly, is the same rental Sir Robert Knolles paid on his town house in Seething Lane. This ceremony is still carried on today, known as Robert Knolles'Rose a red rose is presented to the Lord Mayor of London on mid summers' day.

In the Tudor reign the family is better documented, Robert's eldest son Francis received the same favour under Henry VIII as his father did and was confirmed in the estate of Rotherfield. His marriage to Catherine, daughter of Sir William Carey, in 1514 when she was fifteen, made his future in later years better than he could have imagined.

Sir William Carey had married Mary Boleyn with whom Henry VIII had an affair before he started his liaison with sister Anne. It is reputed that Mary was pregnant with Henry's child when she married William Carey, certainly Carey's first born child, Henry, justified any Plantagenet genes in him with his exploits on the Scottish border when as Lord Hunsdon he was Warden of the West Marches. Francis, as the husband of Queen Elizabeth's first cousin and a strict puritan, Elizabeth had implicit faith in his loyalty knowing that his fortune depended upon her reign and that the last thing he would do would be to plot the usurpation of the Catholic Mary Queen of Scots. Unlike the older aristocracy who could trim their beliefs according to the reign. When Francis was Mary's gaoler in Carlisle Castle even he was struck by her charm.

Earlier, when Mary I had restored Catholicism to England, after the death of Edward VI, Francis took his family to protestant Germany but he returned before Mary's death. Francis was knighted by Edward VI and in 1542 became M.P. for Horsham.

On Elizabeth's accession in 1558 he was made a member of her council and was on many commissions ranging from defence and religion to currency, his town house is said to have been near St.Martin's in the Field. His children had chequered lives, his second but eldest surviving son was William, born in 1547, he was knighted in 1586 and made a lord in 1603. Charles I created him Earl of Banbury in 1626. His first wife having died, he married Elisabeth O-Howard when he was 58 and she 19. His will dated 1630 makes no mention of children and the funeral certificate at the College of Arms states that he died without issue, however the Countess in 1627, when he was 80 gave birth to a son, Edward, at her husband's home, and in 1630-31 had another son, Nicholas, at the residence of Lord Vaux, who she married within five weeks of her husband's death. Although in law they were legitimate when the eldest son tried to take his place in the House of Lords the noble Lords fell about laughing and probably told him the medieval equivalent of 'pull the other one'.

The family contested this and continued to use the title of Earl and calling the eldest son Viscount Wallingford, they finally abandoned the claim in 1813.

In Elizabeth's reign a variant in the spelling of name began to be used, this was Knollys, all three variants were used equally in the state records. This branch began to use Knollys consistently and do so even now. Their descendent today is Viscount Knollys whose grandfather was Edward VII private secretary and I believe was very useful finding safe houses for Teddy to take his women, anyway Edward seemed to think it was worth a Viscountcy. Another branch of the Knolles-Vaux family spelt their name as Knowles, they produced several Admirals one of them serving with Nelson. This family still exist today as Baronets.

Another of Sir Francis Knollys' sons was Henry, he was one of the partners in Sir Humphrey Gilbert's expedition to America in 1578 but he quarrelled with Sir Humphrey and taking three ships out to the Bay of Biscay took to piracy.

Letitia, Sir Francis' daughter, has become the most famous member of the family, having a novel written on her life, being portrayed on television and her son having a Hollywood epic based on his rise and fall.

Letitia Knollys, more commonly known as Lettice, was born in 1541,

one of eleven children of Sir Francis Knollys. Her mother Catherine being the Queen's cousin and friend Lettice was soon a Lady of Honour to the Queen and one of her favourites. In 1561 she married Walter, Viscount Hereford, whose family, the Devereux were descended from the Evereux who arrived with William the Conqueror. It was the usual joining of old blood and new wealth and power, the Devereux could claim descent from the royal Plantagenet's and the best the Knollys could claim was from a soldier of fortune and the worst from a tradesman. There were five children, four of whom lived, her husband spent most of his time trying to suppress rebellion in Ireland where he led an expeditionary force, he had to finance this himself and hope to recoup his money and win himself honour and estates, the Queen loaned him ten thousand pounds at ten per cent to equip his force, this was Elizabeth's usual way of conducting campaigns with insufficient revenue.

Devereux approached the task as a professional soldier making war on barbarians, at one point having invited the rebel leaders to banquet he proceeded to massacre them, civilised behaviour had ceased to exist.

It is probable that it was during her husband's absence in Ireland that Lettice met Robert Dudley, Earl of Leicester, Master of the Queen's Horse and favourite, who has been accused of making sure that Lettices husband was kept in Ireland and clear his way for an affair.

When Devereux, who was created Earl of Essex in 1571, died of dysentery in Ireland there was talk of poison, Leicester was the last person to want Lettice free to marry again he had more ambitious plans to marry Elizabeth. As regards Lettice her motive may been to clear the way to marry Leicester.

Elizabeth's name was linked to Leicester's in scandal through out Europe and when Leicester's wife was found dead at the bottom of a flight of stairs Elizabeth was in danger of losing her throne when both Leicester and herself were rumoured to be accomplices. Although Elizabeth distanced herself from Leicester she was intensely jealous if he showed interest in anyone else so that when Letitia became pregnant and Leicester was forced to marry her in 1578 she was banished from the court.

Letitia's son by her first marriage was the Robert Earl of Essex, who became with the aid of the patronage of his stepfather Leicester, Elizabeth's favourite, portrayed in the film 'Elizabeth and Essex' with Bette Davis and Errol Flynn in the title roles.

Letitia, now the Countess of Leicester, named her son by Leicester after his father making another Robert, he died at the age of six, his tomb is in St.Mary's church Warwick near his parents, he is named on the tomb as 'The Noble Imp'. The marriage soon became acrimonious, some say that when Leicester suspected that Letitia was having an affair with his Gentleman of Horse, he attempted to have him killed while on campaign with him in Holland, but the plot did not succeed.

Leicester died in 1588 of a 'contival fever', although poison was suspected a post- mortem showed nothing, but many stories were circulated one - was that Leicester had given Letitia a poisoned bottle of liquor telling her to use it if she felt faint and she unknowingly gave it to him when he taken ill; another gossip was that he gave her a poisoned drink and she suspecting this switched glasses. Whatever happened Letitia later married Sir Christopher Blount Leicester's Gentleman of Horse.

Robert her son had an adventurous career but never achieved any outstanding success, he led an expedition against Spain and was the first ashore at Cadiz. In 1599 he was given the commission to pacify and re-conquer Ireland, with him was his stepfather Sir Christopher Blount. Essex's Irish campaign was not a success. Tyrone, the Irish rebel leader eluded Essex and the climate made him ill, he dispensed knighthoods liberally to keep up morale which outraged the Queen and finally agreed an ignominious truce with Tyrone. Elizabeth sent express commands not to agree any terms until he had submitted them to her, but by then he had already done so.

Essex was now desperate, some of his friends urged him to march home and seize the court but Blount recommended staying in Ireland. Typically he did neither but landed in England with a few friends and burst in on the Queen unannounced, with his face and clothes still muddy. He found the Queen still not yet dressed and without her wig and make-up, Essex fell on his knees and kissed her hand and was led to believe that he was back in the Queen's favour, but later that evening he was ordered to keep to his room.

The following day the Privy Council drew up a list of charges relating to his conduct of the Irish campaign and his reckless return, he was imprisoned at York Horse where he was held for the next six months, during which time he became seriously ill.

He was released in August 1600 and allowed to go anywhere except the court, deeply in debt he was hoping to keep the tax on the import of wines which was due to expire, the Queen cancelled this and refused to answer his letters. He began to regard his position as untenable and led on by some of his friends he began to gather the disaffected around him, his sister Penelope aided him and visited many of her brother's friends to canvass their support. Later Essex was to accuse her of a much more serious involvement and to suggest that he was goaded on by her beyond his own ambitions.

On the 8th February three hundred armed men gathered in the courtyard of Essex House, but after a brief siege the plotters were taken prisoner, among them was Christopher Blount who was wounded. After his trial, where he was sentenced to death, Essex made a private confession incriminating his associates including his sister. Essex was beheaded on Tower Hill on February 25th 1601 aged 33, Sir Christopher Blount followed on March 5th.

Letitia died on 25th December 1634 aged 94 and is buried with Leicester in a magnificent tomb at Warwick. A novel of Letitia's life, 'My Enemy the Queen' was written by Victoria Holt. The life of Penelope is covered in 'Poor Penelope' by Sylvia Freedman.

Another of the family with local connections is Richard Knolles who was one the earliest masters at Sir Roger Manwood's Grammar School at Sandwich. He was born at Cold Ashby in Northants probably in 1540, his father's name was Francis and was probably a cousin or nephew of Sir Francis Knollys; this branch of the family always spelt the name as Knolles. He graduated at Lincoln College Oxford in 1564-5 and was appointed master of Sandwich Grammar in 1573 at a salary of twenty pounds a year, more than most schools paid and better than the five pounds he was getting as a fellow at Lincoln. He wrote a number of history books while at Sandwich and also translated several others so much so that he neglected his teaching and the governors of the school tried to retire him on a pension but as he was well in with Sir Roger Manwood's son who paid his salary he carried on as he was.

One of his books 'The Generall Historie of the Turkes' was reviewed by Dr.Johnson who made his usual caustic remarks saying *"That it was very good but it would have better if he had written about something interesting"* .

When Coleridge was setting out for Malta, Southey wrote to him *"Look in old Knolles and read the siege of Malta before you go"*. And Byron wrote that *"Knolles was one of the first books that gave me pleasure when I was a child"* .

Although he was a pain in the neck to the school in his lifetime he is now regarded as the most illustrious master the school ever had, with one of the school houses named after him.

In 1610 Richard and four of his children all died between 4th June and 6th July, probably caused by an outbreak of plague, Sandwich was a busy port and would be the first to be affected by continental outbreaks.

His family life appears to be a mystery, according to the local records Richard Knowles M.A. of St.Mary's Sandwich married Mary Best of Margate by License in 1584; but in the parish records of Cold Ashby he married Frances Holmby in 1560 and had several children and Frances is named as his widow in 1613 in the will probate.

To get back to our family, William the younger son who was named in the will of 1435 is just possibly our ancestor.

William was underage in 1435 and the 100 Marks were held in trust by his elder brother Thomas; in the will of Richard Knowles of Gravesend in 1500 he bequeaths goods to his father William who is still living and must be quite elderly. It is possible that this William is the same as the one mentioned in 1435. Richard's brother, who was also mentioned in the will, was named Charles, this is a very unusual christian name at this period, not until the Stuart's came to the throne in the seventeenth century do you find this name at all common. It hints of a connection with France, Gravesend has always been a commercial port and if William had continued the family trade as a merchant he could have traded with France and had a French wife. His nephew Richard was a merchant in London and would be a cousin to his son also named Richard. If William shared his families Lancastrian politics he would have been ideally placed to smuggle in couriers and help refugees escape, perhaps he was the one who carried Cornelius over to England?

Perhaps to confirm this possibility in 1490 a William Knolles was left twenty shillings annually for life in the will of Jane Isgoldisthorpe who owned the manor of Selling and Wickhambreaux, like most landed families their allegiances were undecided with relations in both camps. Her father John Tiptoft, Earl of Worcester, was a Yorkist and married into the Neville family he was commissioned to try all cases of treason summarily without jury and was responsible for many deaths including the Earl of Oxford and his eldest son. When the Neville family, led by the Earl of Warwick, changed sides Tiptoft was handed over to the Lancastrians and tried by John de Vere, Earl of Oxford, whose father and elder brother he had condemned. Jane Isgoldisthorpe's daughter married John Neville who also changed sides and was killed at Barnet, so it is possible that she may have good cause to be grateful for someone who had outlets out of the country.

The Knowles family continued in Gravesend into the seventeenth century with the christian names William, Robert and Richard predominating, which could make it the source of the family in the Birling area.

But without further evidence being unearthed this may never be proved.

Jill Florence Maura Clowes (nee Knowles) 1946 -

Written in 2017

The following information, in support of and adding to the work of William Knowles of Sheerness, comes from several sources. It is taken from family trees on the Ancestry.com site, web sites that list wills, Roots web - Your Heritage page 35088, GENI and Wikipedia.

A **William Thomas Knollys** was born in 1270 in North Mymms Hertfordshire and died in 1330 in Hertfordshire. He married Jane Muir Greenlees and they had a son, Sir Thomas Knollys, born 1290.

Sir Thomas Knollys, born 1290 died 1350. He married Lady Joan (unknown).

Their son was **Sir Robert (Old Brigand) Knollys**, born 1312 at North Mymms Hertfordshire. He died 15th August 1407 at Sculethorpe Manor Norfolk. He married Lady Constance de Beverley. He was a knight of the 100 years war, (well documented in William's original work).

On one occasion, whilst he was away at war, his wife bought a plot of threshing ground opposite their house in Seething Lane, London. She was annoyed at the chaff dust which kept blowing across the lane so decided to plant a rose garden, and had a fourteen feet high footbridge built across the lane to access the rose garden avoiding the muddy road. Unfortunately, she did not obtain the equivalent of today's planning permission and as a penalty had to pay an annual rent of a red rose every June to the Lord Mayor. The rose garden and footbridge are long gone – but the annual rose ceremony still takes place.

More detail about this ceremony later in the book.

Sir Robert Knollys and Sir John Cobham contributed to the cost of the building of a bridge across the River Medway at Rochester in 1391. They also got their wealthy friends, including one Dick Whittington, to contribute to a Bridge Trust for the maintenance of the bridge. Although their bridge was replaced in the Victorian era, the Bridge Trust still exists and one of its functions is to encourage engineering education nationally.

The next generation was **Sir Robert Knollys** (now also recorded as Knolls/Knowles) born 1330 in London, died 1st July 1370 in North Mymms Hertfordshire, thus predeceasing both his parents.

Sir Robert's son was Sir Thomas Knollys (Knolles/ Knowles) 1360 -1435.

Sir Thomas Knowles , 1360– 1435, as referred to in William's work, was twice a Lord Mayor in London 1399 and 1410. He married Jane or Joan (unknown) 1368 – 1435.

They lived at Cordwainer Street London (named after the professional shoemakers who lived in this area). Thomas was an Alderman and a member of the Worshipful Company of Grocers of the City of London. He was named in, and one of the executors of, his grandfather's Will.

In 1391 he purchased a quarter share of the Manor of North Mymms from Beatrix Bakston for 100 marks of silver. Having a country retreat was a great advantage in the summer months when London would have been particularly polluted due to the lack of sanitation.

In 1400/10 he directed the rebuilding of the Guildhall and had the church of St. Antholin's built in Watling Street. He and his wife were buried in that church. Their epitaph stated that he was a grocer, an Alderman for 40 years and twice Lord Mayor. According to the inscription they had 19 children.

St. Antholin's church was in Cordwainer Ward and was destroyed in the Fire of London. The present Cordwainer Street is in the EC2 area of the City of London.

In 1428 he purchased the other ¾ of the Manor of North Mymms from the descendants of Simon Swonlond, making him Lord of the Manor.

The next generation was **Sir Thomas Knollys** 1390 – 1445 born and died in London. He married Isabelle (unknown) in 1405, aged 15. When his father died he inherited the North Mymms Estate but died 10 years later.

In Thomas's will dated 7/8 February 1445 he mentions his wife Isabelle, and his son Robert who inherited the estate. Also mentioned in his will were daughters Beatrice (a nun at Dartford), and Johanna, who married William Baron, and Isabella.

From further church records, accessed from the page 35088 of Roots web, it seems that Robert had 4 children but the 2 sons died young. So eventually the estate was split between the two daughters and therefore went out of the family name on their marriages.

The junior branch of the family continued as there were two other sons of Thomas and Isabelle, Richard and John.

There are only a few details that I can add to William's work about the family in the 17th and 18th century.

The transcript of Thomas Knowles and Elizabeth Knight's marriage can be viewed at the Family History Research centre at Maidstone library.

Their son Richard was baptised 22nd December 1607. He married Katherine Johnson at Leybourne.

Richard and Katherine's son John married Sarah Cox at Snodland 27th November 1676.

John's son William married Mary Cox at Eynsford. His farming and family is detailed in William's work as is his Inventory. The Inventory is a very detailed documentation of the goods and chattels in the house and the animals and farm stock. They are buried together in the Church graveyard at Boughton Aluph.

William and Mary's son John was baptised 13thDecember 1724, he married Mary Attwood 13th January 1747 at Boughton Aluph. He died 3rd February 1774 and is buried at Lynsted. It was John's brother William that moved to and founded the Plaxtol branch of the family- (covered in William's original story).

This was the branch of the family that started to spread from the Ryarsh, Birling, Snodland cluster of villages. This is significant for us because Lynsted is between Faversham and Sittingbourne.

John and Mary's son William was born in Lynsted in 1755, and died in Tunstall, near to Milton Regis, in 1831. He was married to Elizabeth Smeed.

William's Will can be read in the records of the UK Prerogative Court of Canterbury 1384-1858. The script is not the easiest of reads, but it is also quite a complicated document. He leaves his wife Elizabeth household goods and chattels. Also the interest arising from 400 ? 3 ½ p.cent and 300 ? 5 ½ p.cent now in the hands of Mr. John Champion the elder and Mr. Benjamin Champion the younger, residing at the Chest Arms, Chatham – victuallers. This is for her lifetime and thereafter between the lawfully begotten children, both male and female, of his three sons, John, William and Thomas, and of his two daughters, Elizabeth and Anne. It seems that he loaned money for business purposes – a private mortgage arrangement maybe.

The Will goes on to bequeath the Tunstall property with yards, grounds, buildings, freehold to his son William, a gardener at Maidstone, to hold for himself and his heirs. There are further legacies for his wife, also for son Thomas, living at Willesborough, (who predeceased him) and both daughters. These amounts totalled over a thousand pounds. His executors were *"my dear son"* John of Faversham (our ancestor) and Mr. George Southby.

It struck me as rather strange that, unless in my several readings of the will I have missed something, John was not a beneficiary.

John was born in Sittingbourne in 1777, married Ethelinda Hull on the 17th November 1798 at Milton Regis and died there in 1853. They are the first ancestors to be recorded on a Census. In 1841 he is recorded as being 60 years old and living at Plantation, Ospringe Road, Faversham. When we visited Ospringe there is a Plantation Road, so they possibly lived, and he was a market gardener, where a housing estate now stands.

In the 1851 Census they lived at Cross, Milton Regis. There is a Cross Lane at Milton and, at one time, a stone cross and the town pump stood where there is now a green, in the High Street near the Old Court Hall. (Taken from the booklet *"Milton Regis Trial"* published by the Sittingbourne Society, my copy has been corrected by Douglas Knowles the unofficial Mayor of Milton!!)

To pause for a moment and reflect on the eras through which these ancestors lived. When Thomas was mayor of London Richard the Second was king but surrendered his crown to Bolingbroke who became Henry the Forth. The Battle of Agincourt – and people were burnt at the stake for Heresy.

When William *"under 21"* was alive football was banned in Scotland, Eton school was founded, a law was passed regulating mode of dress for each class of person. The Battle of Bosworth, Joan of Arc, and the Princes in the Tower would have all made the headlines, had there been newspapers.

In the time of Thomas Knowles and Elizabeth Knight, Elizabeth the First was queen, Sir Francis Drake circumnavigated the world, the Spanish Armada, Sir Walter Raleigh and Mary Queen of Scots would have been the news of that era. Shakespeare was writing plays, Guy Fawkes tried to blow up Parliament and London merchants were becoming wealthier and grander than some titled gentry. Just before Thomas died in 1623, King James the First decreed that nobles and gentry should *"quit their frivolities of London and fashion and return to their duties on their estates!"*

Richard Knowles and Katherine Johnson would have lived through the reign of Charles 1, civil war and the Commonwealth/Protectorate under Cromwell. Van Dyke, Inigo Jones and William Harvey were plying their professions.

John Knowles and Sarah Cox saw the Restoration of the monarchy and the Great Fire of London.

William and Mary at Boughton Aluph lived through the reigns of William and Mary, Queen Anne, George the First and George the Second. The Battle of Blenheim, the South Sea Bubble, and Edmund Halley's appointment as Royal Astronomer would have been headlines. Handel composed The Water Music.

John and Mary in the 1700s – may have known that Canaletto visited London, and a new song had been written that became the National Anthem. Mozart and Wedgewood were well known, and Kew became a centre of Botanical Research – all in the reign of George the Third.

William and Elizabeth 1755-1831, would have heard about the scandals surrounding the Prince Regent and the building of the Brighton Pavilion -Nelson defeating Napoleon at Trafalgar, Wellington's triumph at Waterloo, the French Revolution and George the Fourth becoming king.

During the lives of John Knowles and Ethelinda Hull William the Fourth came to the throne before the long reign of his niece Victoria. The Great Exhibition at Crystal Palace was 2 years before our ancestor John died.

From here on relevant history becomes almost modern.

To pick up the thread again with John Knowles and Ethelinda Hull, (she was the daughter of Thomas Hull and Lydia Jackson), they had 13 children as far as I can ascertain from the various available records. Several of them died in infancy, Sophia, the first Lydia, Elizabeth, Charles, Sarah, another Lydia, Ethelinda and Richard.

Their daughter Mary Ann, born 1807, married William Parker in 1826. They stayed in Milton and had five daughters, Ellen, Sarah Jane, Sophia, Elizabeth and Ester.

Their son Thomas, born 1812, married Elizabeth and their son was called John, it seems that Thomas died in London.

John and Ethelinda's son John, born 1814, married Ann Martin at Chatham in 1833 and Ann Epps at Faversham in 1845. There were several children from both marriages. A census shows him as a labourer, another as a shoe maker. He died in 1860 on the Isle of Sheppey.

John and Ethelinda's son William was baptised 7/7/1816 at Milton Church, married Sarah Jane Stillwell 6/8/1838 at St. Mary's church Lambeth. Their children were Ethelinda born 1839 and Jane Caroline born 1840. Sarah died in 1841.

In 1842 he married Catherine Walker at St. Mary's church Newington Southwark. They had three children Sarah 1844, Eliza Salome 1849, and Catherine 1851 – she died in 1930.

Our ancestor was Edward, born 13/06/1802 – the eldest son of John Knowles and Ethelinda Hull. He died 9th April 1877 and is buried at Milton Regis.

At this stage much of the family history is recorded. William's original story tells of Edward's work as a gardener, a victualler at the Shipwright's Arms on Milton Quay, which at that time would have been a very busy area, and a seed merchant. All that I can usefully add is some information about the properties the family occupied at the dates of censuses, their occupations where shown, and who the children of Edward and Mary Wildish married.

The 1841 census records the family at Pound Row Milton Regis which no longer exists. The children of Edward and his wife Mary Wildish were John aged 13, Amy 9, Edward 5, Sarah 3 and William 3 months. I have found that not all children are included on all census records. The eldest daughter, Ethelinda born 11/06/1826, I found on a separate census – aged 15 and living with grandparents John and Ethelinda Knowles.

The 1851 census shows the family at 46 High Street Milton, which is a very small terraced house on the hilly part of the High Street. It describes Edward as a seed merchant and the children are Edward aged 14 (a labourer), Sarah 12, William 6 (?) and Susannah 5 all described as students. Also Susannah Kemp –sister- place of birth Faversham, which probably means that she was Mary Wildish's married sister visiting the family. I understand that the Seed Shop was further up the High Street in a property which is still there a few doors along from the High House towards the Three Hats public house.

By the time of the 1861 Census the only child still at home was Susannah aged 15.

The 1871 census shows Edward, as a widower, living alone at 65 St. Paul's Street Milton Regis which is at the bottom end of Milton High Street and although the road is still there the area has been redeveloped. I have a post card of the area as it would have been at that time showing a shop on the corner with children playing outside.

Before moving on to our direct ancestor Edward, born 26/06/1836, some details about his siblings starting with John Wildish Knowles.

John married Susanna Horton in 1852, and a year after she died in 1882 he married Frances Ann Beal.

The children of John Wildish Knowles and Susanna Horton were Thomas Knowles Horton born 1852 and died in 1932 in Newcastle-upon-Tyne. His three children were John Thomas, Annie and Ethel Linda.

John and Susanna's eldest daughter was Mary Ann born 1853. On the 1861 census she is a scholar living at the family home at 27 Bridge Street, her father's occupation, a Mariner. On the 1881 census she is a school mistress living at 56 Charlotte Street with her mother. By the 1891 Census she is still a school mistress living at 56 Charlotte Street but her father is now married to Frances Beal. Mary Ann died in February 1900 and her step-mother died later that year in June.

John and Susanna's next daughter was Susan Ann born 30/01/1855. The record of a burial of Susan Ann Knowles exists on CLDS site dated 30/09/1856 at Milton Regis. Whilst the record does not give details of next of kin, I am as certain as I can be that this is the same Susan Ann as there are no further mentions of her in censuses or BDM records.

John and Susanna's next child was a son born September 1856, died 1876 aged 19. He was followed by John Wildish born 1863 and William John Wildish born 1864. Both boys died within a year of their births.

I have a letter written to Douglas Knowles in 1975 by a Dorothy Kemp, nee Knowles, with a home address in Newcastle on Tyne. She is enquiring about relations of her father, John Thomas Knowles, and enclosed copies of letters written to him by his grandfather, John Wildish Knowles, when her father lived in Newcastle. She wanted to know the connection with the name Horton.

We have copies of a birth certificate recording Thomas Knowles born 12th. February 1852, mother Susanna Horton, father's name not recorded.

A marriage certificate dated 25th. December 1875 between Thomas Knowles Horton (mariner) and Annie Lillie (residence at time of marriage, Stockton) in the presence of J W Knowles and M A Knowles.

Also, a birth certificate for John Thomas Knowles, born 11.35am 30th. August 1880 at King Street Milton Regis, mother Annie Horton, formally Lilley, father Thomas Knowles Horton (Barge Master).

The surname seems to have been amended but, as she wrote that her father had died in 1947 aged 67 – the link could be made.

The copied letters all begin *"Dear Grandson"*, and end *"your affectionate grandfather J W Knowles"*, all written from 56 Charlotte Street Milton Regis, a terraced house which still exists, between April 1904 and August 1905. An image of Milton Regis church is on the top of each letter.

One letter tells of how poorly he has been, taking to his bed for 3 weeks. He says that aunt Amy has also been poorly, so hasn't written, and couldn't take her beer, but hoped to by the time he visits them again. His brother

Ted's corn does not seem much better but they are all fairly well in Hythe Road.

Another letter is equally woeful – sorry to hear his father has been *"sadly"*, and hopes he will be better soon. Sorry to hear about Susan and hope the Lord will spare her for the sake of her children. Aunt Amy still very sadly and hasn't left the house since September (letter dated 10/4/04). He says he is better but cannot get up the top of the street and doesn't expect to gain strength again at his age but thank God his appetite is good. He tells his grandson that a local boy, John Williamson, has gone to Canada on the *"Victorian"* and has arrived safely. Also, that his brother Edward is very worried about his daughter Polly being so ill, but they are all "nicely" up at the PO and send best wishes.

The other letter is a bit more cheerful – he is feeling much better and was able to get to church for the first time since September – they are looking forward to his visit and will make him as comfortable as possible – Aunt Amy is better, *"him being ill nearly broke her"* – their granddaughter Lizzie (the recipient's sister) had stayed with them the week before and was very comfortable with them – he has not seen Mrs. Horace since they moved to Chestnut House but knows she is not enjoying good health, they were hoping that the move to such a pleasant house in the country would do her good. (He was referring to my grandmother, Matilda Jane Knowles, who died two years after the letter was written at the age of 37). Chestnut House is at Chestnut Street between Sittingbourne and Newington. A very pretty country house now made into two dwellings in an area of very nice old properties some of which I think are listed.

The aunt Amy referred to in the letters seems to be living with her brother John. However apart from the listing of her on the 1841 census as a 9 year old daughter of Edward and Mary I haven't been able to establish any further information.

Edward and Mary seem to have had three daughters all named Mary Ann.

The first was born in December 1827 and died in January 1828.

The second was born 28/09/1834 and died in August 1836.

The third Mary Ann was born 11/02/1844 and according to records, baptised the same day. I have been unable to establish any further information about her from any source other than her baptismal record.

Edward and Mary's son William born 1841 died in 1862. He was drowned in the river aged 21 and is buried in Milton Regis churchyard.

Susannah (various spellings depending on the record), was born in 1846 and married Thomas Bayly 27/8/1866 and had 4 children with him - Thomas William, Mary Knowles, Edwin Thomas and George who died in infancy. Her husband died and she married John Benjamin Ashcroft at Dover. They had 3 children, John, George and Elizabeth Mary. Susannah died in 1904, the death certificate showing cause of death as heart disease and oedema of the lungs.

Edward and Mary's daughter Sarah Ann born 7/10/1838, married George Moore on 28/5/1862 at Milton Regis. Their children were Harriet, William, George James, Edward Thomas, Sarah Ann and John Wildish. On the 1871 census George's occupation is a mariner with the home address as 28 St. Paul's Street Milton Regis. On the 1881

Census the family is still at 28 St. Paul's Street, and George is described as a Waterman on board *"Henry and Elizabeth"* with other crew members named Shrubshall – a name still well known in Milton at the time that I worked at the PO. On the 1891 Census Sarah Ann is living at 31 Havelock Street, St Mary Northgate Canterbury and described as *"living on own means"*. She has visitors recorded on the census named Beaney – again a Milton name I was familiar with when working at the PO.

I do not know if there is any connection but a family named Beaney bought a greengrocer's shop in Mortimer Street Herne Bay that was previously owned by a member of the Knowles family.

Edward and Mary's eldest daughter was Ethelinda, born in 11/06/1826. She married William Wells on 13/10/1853 and they had 3 children, Emma 1854, Harry 1863, and Arthur 1866. From the Census records she appears to have moved around quite a bit. 1861 – Milton Regis: 1871- Blue Town Sheppey: 1881 Minster: 1891- 4, Pigtail Minster: 1901 Minster: and place of death on 9/10/1908 is recorded as Sheppey.

Edward Knowles 1836-1917 was my great grandfather and great great grandfather to Edward and Ivan – and we seem to share that privilege with a great many other descendants!!

A lot has been written about Edward in William's original story and in various publications. The local Sittingbourne Gazette made him the subject of one of their *"Peep Shows of the Past"* articles. The article is reproduced later in this book. It made much of his business acumen, particularly when dealing with the auctioneers at the London markets, his wit and sense of humour and his service to the local community.

In October 2010 The Archive magazine published an article on the early sub-postmasters of Milton and hailed him as the founder of a three generation *"dynasty"*.

I will briefly summarize the facts as I know them and leave others to add their own knowledge – or correct mine!

Born in 1836 to Edward and Mary Knowles who lived at Pound Row at the time. Father Edward was a gardener and seed merchant.

The family moved to 46 High Street Milton Regis by the time of the 1851 census. He rang the curfew bell for his father – the last boy to do so before the custom was abolished. It is said he knew a great deal of the gossip/news of the town even at a young age – dinner table chat apparently.

He married Mary Ann Wiles, daughter of William Wiles and Frances Pankhurst, in 1858.

His first business was a bakery at 87 High Street to which he added a PO in 1865. He moved the business across the street in about 1870 to numbers 64-66 and added a greengrocery shop to the bakery and PO. He and his family lived at 46 Albion Terrace, now Brewery Road just behind the Court Hall.

The High Street shops are all still there and identifiable. The house in Albion Terrace is less easy to identify. The end wall of the Terrace still has the name Albion visible – although the bricks have been painted over. The row of houses that remain have been renumbered so it is impossible to say exactly which one the family lived in – or even if some of the Terrace has been demolished.

The censuses confirm all addresses and the businesses – listing him as SPM, Civil servant and two daughters as PO clerks.

The 1901 census shows him and Mary visiting their son Charles and family in Scotland. The 1911 census shows him living at *"Blenheim"* Sittingbourne still listed as SPM and fruiterer.

Blenheim House, London Road Sittingbourne is now a dental practice but the frontage is little changed from Edward and Mary's time. A photograph of Edward and his second wife, Margaret, taken on the front steps of the house in 1914 bears witness to the fact.

His last business acquisition was in 1906 when he bought a building and contracting company from WJ Beaumont. There is a connection here to the man his daughter Margaret married and emigrated to Canada with.

His public service included School Attendance Officer for 39 years: Bailiff of the Manor of Milton: Town Crier and Deacon of the Milton Congregational Church.

The first two offices were continued by his son Horace Sparkes Knowles who also took over as Sub Postmaster when Edward retired – I understand there was a continuation of interest in all business matters almost until his death.

His wife Mary died in 1903 and two years later he married Margaret Alice Potter, his late wife's sister. The marriage took place in Jersey as it was not legally possible to marry your sister-in-law in England at the time. I have a letter written by his daughter Mary to a cousin that speaks of the *"Guvnor,"* as he was generally known, being in Jersey preparing for the wedding. She goes on to talk of the boys playing football in the yard and Horace being at Iwade where he had orchards.

Edward died in 1917 and probate was granted to his sons Charles and Horace. His estate was worth £4162-17-3.

Edward and Mary had 13 children.

I will list the ones first who sadly did not survive.

Twins Frances and Ethelinda born 1859 – died 1859.

Sydney born 1873 - died 1873. Harry born 1877 – died 1877

Emma Agnes born 1879 – died 1880.

The surviving children were Edward born 1860: Mary Ann born 1863: Margaret Alice born 1864: William born 1866: James Pankhurst born 1867: Horace Sparkes born 1870: Charles born 1871: Bernice Harriet born 1875.

Mary Ann Wiles father was William Wiles, a brick maker, and her mother was Frances Pankhurst.

Mary's siblings were brothers William, Horace, Charles, James and John and sisters Frances, Emily, Margaret Alice and Agnes.

Thus, some Christian names new to the Knowles family were influenced by the Wiles family.

Edward 1860 – 1930

I am leaving Edward and his descendants in the more knowledgeable hands of his great grandsons Ivan and Edward.

Material that I have to share includes:

A Red exercise book of childhood memories of her grandparents Edward and Ann Knowles of Faversham written by Muriel Dell whose mother was their daughter Annie.

Copies of "Bygone Kent" with articles about Edward's business in Faversham and related accounts of his council activities.

Copies of photographs of Edward and sons Charles and Harry in open top motor cars.

Newspaper article which includes the *"Water pump"* story.

A photograph taken in Sittingbourne in 1952 when Harry Knowles was Mayor of Faversham. He and his wife, Nellie, were Guests of Honour at the Sittingbourne Urban District Council Annual Dinner Dance – the Chairman of the Council being Douglas Knowles JP.

Also, the evening's music/dance programme and menu.

Photographs of Muriel Dell with her mother Annie and Grandmother Ann Knowles.

A photo of the grandchildren of Edward's son Harry and his wife Nellie taken at their Golden Wedding Celebration in 1972.

Mary Ann Knowles 1863- 1941.

Mary Ann was known to her nieces and nephews as Aunt Polly. Polly being the usual aka for Mary Anns – I am told.

In the 1881 Census she is listed as Postmaster's daughter aged 18 living at 56/58/60 High Street Milton. By the 1891 Census she is a PO Clerk. In the 1901 census she is resident at *"Blenheim"*, her parent's house, with her younger sister Bernice and Bernice's husband Andrew Willson and their baby Mary Ann Knowles Willson. Edward and Mary were in Scotland at this time with their son Charles and his family.

My sister, Mary Jean Sinclair nee Knowles, remembers Aunt Polly quite well. She was taken to see her as a young child and it seems she was often in bed *"poorly"*. The concern about her health was mentioned in one of the letters that John Wildish Knowles (brother to Edward and therefore uncle to Polly) wrote to his grandson in Newcastle in 1904/05.

She was a talented seamstress – as were many girls at that time – and she made white table cloths for each of the nephews and nieces when they got married. The cloths were a mixture of drawn thread work and crocheted edges with a large embroidered K in one corner. To my knowledge at least two of those still exist – and are sometimes carefully used!

There are at least two photos of her – one at her younger sister's wedding, and another sitting on a swing in a garden, probably at the rear of *"Blenheim"*.

When my sister was taken to see Aunt Polly she had to sit on a low wooden chair with a tapestry seat, normally used as a nursing chair. When Aunt Polly died she left Mary

Jean, daughter of Stuart Knowles, and therefore her great niece, the chair and her watch.

Aunt Polly died 6/07/1941 at the house in Crown Road, Milton Regis where she had lived alone, as far as we know, after her parent's deaths.

Edward and Mary's second daughter was **Margaret Alice Knowles 1864-1932.**

The 1871 Census lists her as 6 years old and living at High Street Milton Regis. The 1881 Census – aged 16, Postmaster's daughter at 56/58/60 High Street.

27/01/1890 Margaret married Harry Gardler at Medway.

1891 Census, married to Harry Gardler, a builder's manager for W.Beaumont, living at 12 Crown Road Milton Regis. George Gardler aged 73 lived at 13 Crown Road.

W. Beaumont is the building contractors that Edward, Margaret's father, acquired in 1906.

1901 Census Margaret and Harry are living at 20 Chalkwell Road Milton Regis and have two children Marjorie and Harry.

1911 Census the family are living at 34 Sangley Road Catford SE and Harry's occupation is listed as *"Domestic Bazaar"*. Apparently Domestic Bazaar was a chain of shops selling inexpensive household goods.

The Outward Passenger List for the Cunard ship *"Andania"* leaving Southampton for Quebec on the 25/09/1913 lists Margaret, wife: Marjorie, daughter and a governess: Harold aged 11: Rosalind aged 10: Donald aged 8.

There is a photograph of the family waving farewell from the ship's rail.

Margaret is on the Incoming Passenger list of the *"Aurania"* on the 1st October 1928 from Quebec to London and seems to have spent about 10 months in the UK. She is on the Outward Passenger List on the " *Aurania"* 6/07/1929 arriving back in Montreal 14/07/1929 – as far as I can see she was travelling alone.

Margaret died 7/01/1932 in Victoria BC and is buried in the Royal Oak Burial Park. Harry died in 1946 and is buried at the Mount Pleasant Cemetery Edmonton Alberta.

There are several photos of Margaret and Harry, plus a scan of their marriage certificate on Ancestry's web site.

Margaret and Harry Gardler's children were Marjorie 1890-1966: Harry 1900-1980: Rosalind 1903-1996 and Donald 1905-1983.

Marjorie Gardler is recorded on the 1911 Census as being a governess at a private school at 2, Bouverie Road Folkestone Kent.

Two years later she emigrated to Canada with her family as previously noted.

She married Charles B. Cox in 1919 in Edmonton Alberta. He was born in Balham England. Their children were Raymond B. Cox 1922-2000, he died in Nanaimo BC: Kenneth C. Cox 1925-1995, he died at Nanoose Bay BC: Phylis Cox who I have no details of.

Marjorie died in 1966.

Harry Gardler junior born 1900 in Milton Regis emigrated with his family 1913 and married Queenie Elizabeth Dutton in 1936 in Edmonton Alberta. Their children were Marjorie Gardler born 1937 who married Dave Rous and had a daughter Leah: Betty Gardler born 1941 who married Jim Reheiser.

Harry made a trip to England in 1958 and visited Douglas and Doris Knowles at Milton PO. He gave them gifts of a Canadian Rockies design tablecloth and a pair of porcelain deer which our daughter Katherine now has.

Harry died in 1980 in Edmonton.

Rosalind Gardler born 1903 Milton Regis emigrated with her family 1913 and married Dallas William Borthwick Skillen in Victoria BC in 1925. Their daughter Peggy born 1927 married Harry Wolf and had two children Cheryl and Dallas.

We have had several contacts with Dallas through emails and Skype.

In 1930 she is recorded as living in Snohomish Washington State: in 1947 her address is 885 North Walnut San Jose California.

Rosalind died in 1996 in Calaveras County California but is buried in Ross Bay Cemetery Victoria BC.

There are numerous photos, certificates and pictures of burial stones on Ancestry for many of the above mentioned.

The youngest child of Margaret Knowles and Harry Gardler was Donald, born in 1905, Milton Regis. He emigrated with his family in 1913 and married Caroline (aka Carrie) Dunn in 1930 in Victoria BC. They are recorded as living in Nanaimo in 1935 and again in 1949. In 1962 they were living in Esquimalt Saanich BC.

Their children were Ronald George Gardler born 1931 who married Barbara Joan Simpson. Their children are Karen Marie born 1958: Janice Arlene born 1960: and Wayne Andrew born 1965 – all in Victoria BC.

Ronald died in 2005.

The daughter of Donald Gardler and Carrie Dunn is Patricia Carolyn Gardler born 1937.

Carolyn married Clarence Otto Christensen in 1963 and they have three children.

Carolyn worked for Air Canada and Clarence has now retired from his Law firm.

Clarence and Carolyn visited us in September 2013 and we spent a week visiting both Knowles and Gardler sites around the Sittingbourne, Milton, Sheppey, Rochester area.

Their elder son is David Otto Christensen born 1966 in Calgary. He married Ingrid Anderson in 1989 in Blenheim New Zealand. (coincidence!). Their children are Zachary born 1996 and Benjamin born 1998 in Calgary. David is a professional photographer for the Canadian Government.

Their younger son Paul Donald Christensen was born 1967 in Calgary and married Gudrun Schmidt in Bruhl, Germany in 1992. Their children are Sophie born 1998 and Jacob born 2001 both in Bruhl. Paul is a translater for the German Government and Gudrun is a lawyer. We had the pleasure of meeting Paul in France.

The daughter of Carolyn and Clarence is Lisa Caroline Christensen born 1970. She married Darren Craig Wilton in 1994 in Victoria BC. Their children are Cassidy born 2000 and Charlie born 2003 – they were born in Seattle where the family still live.

We have photos of the above Canadian families - thanks to Carolyn and Clarence.

William Knowles 1866 -1948

William was the fourth child of Edward Knowles and Mary Ann Wiles.

On the 1891 Census he appears as living at 56/58/60/ High Street Milton Regis and is the Postmaster's son.

He married Harriet Ann Ackhurst (1867 – 1942) in 1890 at Milton Regis.

On the 1911 Census they are living at Charlton House Canterbury Road Sittingbourne and his occupation is Fruit Merchant.

At the time of the 1911 Census their eldest son William, born 1891, was listed as a boarder at 166 Invicta Road Sheerness, occupation Florist.

Their other children listed on the Census were: Emily born 1893: Harry born 1895: Hubert born 1899: Stanley born 1903: Hilda Mary born 1905: Margaret born 1908 and Frank born 1910. Also listed is Abram Ackhurst – relative aged 83, probably Harriet's father.

There was another son Robert born 1901 died 1903.

William and Harriet's eldest son William (1891-1964) married Kate Eva Honey (1889-1943) in 1916 on the Isle of Sheppey. They had two children: Edna born 1920 died 1985: William Albert born 1925 died 2001. Neither Edna nor William married. They lived together at Halfway Sheerness and William had two greengrocer shops on the Island. William sold his businesses and retired early. He then spent 16 years investigating various sources of family history information. Some of his travels are detailed in his original notes. Most importantly, it was William whose research, and his generosity in sharing all of it with me, prior to the benefits of the Internet, gave so much information, documents, and photos to the extended family.

William was found collapsed in his home and a letter from me that the police found in the house led them to ask me to go to the hospital, which I did. William died a few days later, his estate going to an animal charity. I told the police about closer relatives than I and asked Marguerite, his cousin, (see Emily's family below) if I could have any family history material that was found when the house was cleared and that I would happily donate to the animal sanctuary. Sadly, I think solicitors dealt with the clearance and Estate and I heard no more.

William and Harriet's daughter Emily married Alfred Hall in 1918. Their children were Marguerite Hall born 1920. She married G.Hammond, they did not have any children. It was Marguerite that I met at her home in Bell Road Sittingbourne who gave me the wedding photo of Bernice Knowles to copy and identified her mother Emily as one of the bridesmaids also putting names to other members of the family. She also gave me a couple of other family wedding groups where the Knowles, Ackhurst and Hall families are identified. However, the copy quality is poor, but may be worth trying to enhance and use.

The second child of Emily and Alfred Hall was Jeanne born 1924. She married Dennis Jarrett in 1954 and they had two children – David born 1962 and Susan Miranda born 1965 both in Chatham. (These last two entries have been difficult to confirm but I believe to be accurate).

Emily and Alfred Hall's only son Robert was born in 1923 and killed in 1944.

William and Harriet's next son was Harry born 1895. On the 1911 Census he is already listed as being an assistant fruiterer. He married Daisy Olive Mitchell (1896-1976) in 1916. Their children were/are Harry Robert Knowles 1916-1942: Peter 1924-2002: Derek 1931 and Diana 1934.

Harry Robert married Elsie E. I. Gilbert in 1941. He died in 1942 and is listed on the WW11 Civilian Deaths Register. His probate seems to have been granted in Llandudno and he is buried at Woodlands Cemetery Gillingham Kent.

Harry and Daisy's second son was Peter born 1924 Sittingbourne and died 2002 Gravesend. I could find no trace of a marriage or children.

Harry and Daisy's third son Derek born 1931 and may have married Kathleen Jolliffe in 1953. I have checked on Ancestry and CLDS and this seemed the most likely recorded marriage given that any tree entries would be protected by the living relative privacy law. I did meet Derek briefly a couple of times at Sub-postmasters' Federation meetings at Canterbury. His PO was in Ashford I think.

Harry and Daisy's only daughter is Diana born 1934. She married Baden A. J. Bedelle (AKA Jim) in 1959 and they had a PO at Kennington Ashford Kent. When Douglas Knowles wanted to retire from Milton Regis PO in 1970 he offered it to Diana and Jim as it was his wish to try and keep the office in the Knowles family – even if not directly. Jim collapsed and died in 1991 and Diana took over the appointment and continued at the office for several years.

They have a son Ian William Bedelle born 1966 and soon after taking over from Douglas in 1970 they had another child – a daughter I believe.

William Knowles and Harriet Ackhurst's next son was Hubert born 1897 died 1973 in Chatham Kent. In the 1901 Census he was living at 20 High Street and by the 1911 Census at Charlton House Sittingbourne although his name is given as Hubert/ Herbert. He married Gladys Ivy Cornwell in 1920 and they had two children.

Their daughter Peggy born 1921 died 1985 appears not to have married. Both Birth and Death are recorded.

Their son Hubert was born 1926 and died in Chatham in 1995. He married June Wise in 1952 in Sittingbourne and they had two children. A daughter Lynn M Knowles born 1954 – she married Mark M Hyland: and a son Richard F H Knowles who married twice – at least the records show two marriages to what seems to be the same Richard F H – Susan C Jordan in 1983 and Donna M E Stone in 1994. (I have not been able to trace whether there are children from either Lynn or Richard without knowledge of Christian names).

The next son of William Knowles and Harriet Ackhurst was Stanley born 1903 died 1987 in the district of Swale.

In the 1911 Census he is living at Charlton House aged 8. In 1928 he married Violet Hubbard at Milton Regis. They had three children: Yvonne born 1931 at Milton Regis: John born 1933 and Anita born 1937.

Yvonne Knowles married David J Orpin in 1959.

Stanley and Violet's son John married Sheila J George in 1957, he died in 1997.

Anita J Knowles born 1937 married Brian J Whelan in 1955 in Sheppey. This confirms the information that Ivan told me that we are distantly related to the family Whelan who own the business on the Isle of Sheppey that produces cement garden items.

Anita and Brian have a son, Andre.

The next child of William and Harriet Knowles was a daughter Hilda Mary born 1905 in Bexley and died 1995 in Gravesend. In the 1911 Census she lives at Charlton House. In 1928 she married Ferdinand William Sander whose parents were Gustav Henry Sander and Hewig Elizabeth Sander married in Germany.

Ferdinand was born in Bexley in 1904 and died there in 1982.

Ferdinand and Hilda's names are on the incoming passenger list aboard the "Carinthia" from Montreal in 1959. Ferdinand was also on an Incoming New York passenger list but I do not have the details.

In 1963 they are recorded on the London Electoral list as living at 63 Lesley Close, Parkhurst Road Bexley.

Hilda Knowles and Ferdinand Sander had two children. Mary born 1934 and registered in Southwark: Michael K. Sander born 1933 and registered in Dartford.

The name Mary Sander brought up several options for marriages that could have fit the time line – so no further information at this stage on Mary.

The same applies to Michael K Sanders – except he is on an Incoming passenger list in 1954 aboard *"The Empress of France"* from Montreal.

It is of course possible that either, or both of them, married abroad.

The next daughter of William Knowles and Harriet Ackhurst was Margaret born 1908 died 1996 in Chatham Kent. In the 1911 Census she is living at Charlton House. She married Sydney French (1908-1978) in 1933 at Milton Regis.

They had four children Robert born 1939 died 1944.

Paul born 1935: David Sydney born 1945 and Margaret A French born 1947.

Because once again Paul French and Margaret French are fairly common names I cannot with any certainty detail their marriages. The difficulty with confirming family groups and links at this stage is the fact that after 1911 census lists are not available.

David Sydney French born 1945 in Chatham married Jane D Smith in 1971 in Bromley and died in 2012 in Gillingham Kent. There is an entry in the Daily Times Index 1995 – current US dated 17/02/2012.

The last child of William Knowles and Harriet Ackhurst is Frank born 1910 in Sittingbourne and died 1997 in Chatham. In the 1911 Census he is living at Charlton House. In 1932 he married Violet Kathleen Mansfield (1910-1979) in Queenborough Sheppey. They had three children Michael F Knowles born 1933 in Milton Regis: Anthony B Knowles born 1938 and Sandra P Knowles born 1944 in Sittingbourne.

Having checked the marriages on Ancestry and CLDS site I have only found three possibilities with the same Christian names and middle initials – so with a fair amount of confidence – Michael married Margaretta B Spence in 1975 in Thanet : Anthony married Sheila J Hayes in 1964 in Chatham : Sandra married Jeremy P Cannan in 1964 in Maidstone.

I have a newspaper article, without date, describing the family of Mr. And Mrs. William Knowles of Charlton House having taken over the *"Bull Hotel"* Sittingbourne for the Christmas period as the family is now too large to accommodate at home.

It talks of the family fruit business and that the family refuses to think of anything as impossible and always look forward! It goes on to list Mr. And Mrs. Knowles guests – five sons and three daughters with their respective spouses– William of Sheerness and two children: Harry and four children: Hubert and two children who live at Dalbyville Bell Road: Stanley and two children: Frank and one child: Mr and Mrs Hall and three children: Mr and Mrs Sanders of Bexley and three children: Mr and Mrs. French of Gillingham: and Frank's mother-in-law Mrs Mansfield. Apparently, William and family took over the hotel for two days and a good time was had by all.

James Pankhurst Knowles

James was the son of Edward Knowles and Mary Ann Wiles born 1867 in Milton Regis. His middle name was taken from his maternal grandmother Frances Pankhurst. In the 1881 census, aged 13, he is living with the family at Milton Regis High Street. He married Charlotte Longley (born 1866) in 1889.

In the 1901 Scotland Census they are living at 34 Gladstone Place, St. Machar Aberdeen with four children. James Charles born 1891: Charlotte Mary born 1893: Sidney born 1897: and Sarah Ellen born 1898. James's occupation is described as fruiterer.

Ten years later the family are on the 1911 Irish Census at 23 Terenure Park Dublin. In addition to the four children already mentioned, and still living at home, are Arthur Malfour born 1905: and Percy Durland born 1908. James's occupation listed as fruit salesman.

It would seem, that when father Edward decided to expand his business interests into Scotland that both James and Charles went north. Even though James and family were in Ireland by 1911 the brothers must still have been in a business partnership because there is a business gazette entry in the early 1930s dissolving the partnership but with both businesses continuing independently of each other – one in Scotland the other in Ireland.

The Dublin shops were damaged during the 1916 uprisings, photos exist showing smashed windows. Compensation was eventually payed and they continued trading.

There is a burial plot at Kilternen Church in Dublin with the following inscriptions:

James Pankhurst Knowles died 1 July 1944 aged 77.

Charlotte wife of James died 11 October 1959 aged 94.

Charlotte, daughter of James and Charlotte, died 28 November 1988 aged 95.

Sarah Ellen, daughter of James and Charlotte, died 14 January 1992.

The four sons of James and Charlotte all married and had families. In William's original work there is a list of names with very few dates or locations. I have taken his information and verified and added to it, where possible, from the Irish records on Ancestry.com and a couple of church sites.

(There is a separate section in this book written by Barry Matthew Knowles the son of Dudley Knowles and Ursula McDermott which will clarify family groups I am sure).

James and Charlotte's son James Charles born 1891 in Aberdeen married Polly O'Reilly. (From William's work). I found a marriage recorded in 1912 between a James Charles Knowles and Esther M F O'Reilly. The children of that marriage were James Charles William known as Jimme: Albert: Brendan: John: Paul: and Sheila. (As listed by William).

Jimme was born 7th. July 1913 at 20, Ashdale Road, Terenure, Dublin. He died in September 1983 in Ealing Middlesex.

Jimme married Sarah A Magan and they had four children all born in Hammersmith London. James in 1942, Michael in 1943, Maureen in 1944 and Patricia in 1946.

The elder son James born 1942 married Phyliss and they had three daughters, Gwendolyn, Kerri and Jennifer.

Brendan Knowles 1918-1969 son of James and Polly, married Teresa Derbyshire and they had four children. Wendy born 1946, Judith born 1947, Brendan born 1949 and Gregory born 1949. Wendy was born in Lancashire, Judith in Surrey and the two sons in Middlesex.

The second son of James and Charlotte was Sydney born 1897 in Aberdeen. He married Mildred Strouts and they had a son Dudley born 1929, died 1996.

Dudley married Ursula McDermott 1932-2014. They had two children, Karen born 1959 and Barry born 1964.

The third son of James and Charlotte was Arthur Malfour Knowles born 1905 in Aberdeen. He married Gertrude Mary Field in 1931 in Dublin. I could only find one child of the marriage – as did William – Shirley born 1936. I could not find a marriage for Shirley so without a surname further checking was not possible. However, William has listed her children as Denep: Shauna: Geraldine: Keiron: Kevin: Branagh: and Stephen. I did wonder if Denep was her husband's name but could not find any records.

The fourth son of James and Charlotte was Percy Durland Knowles born 1907 in Aberdeen. He married Florence Lillian Mitchell in 1936. That marriage confirmed on CLDS site. They had two children Cecelia born 1943 and Nigel born 1938. These also confirmed. William has listed Cecilia's two children as Stewart and Tanya – unable to confirm because no surname. Nigel also had two children Geoffrey and Susanna.

There is a headstone in St. Patrick's Church Enniskerry co Wicklow commemorating Percy Durland Knowles who died 27 February 2001 and his wife Florence who died 7 February 198?.

As previously stated, I believe Barry's section of this book will add to the Irish branch's information.

Horace Sparkes Knowles

Son of Edward Knowles and Ann Wiles. His middle Christian name remains a mystery with no connection to a family surname or obvious reason. There was a famous cricketer at the time called George Sparkes, so maybe Edward was a fan of cricket – who knows!

Horace was born in 1870 in Milton Regis and at the 1881 Census he lived at 56-60 High Street, Postmaster's son and scholar.

In 1889 he married Laura Cavell who came from Ramsgate. In the 1891 Census they were living at 48 Chalkwell Road Milton Regis and had a son Horace Francis Knowles, born 1890. In 1893 their daughter Laura Christina Lavinia was born.

In 1894 his wife Laura died aged 27, leaving him with two small children.

To complete the history of that part of his family before moving on – Horace Francis went to Canada aboard the *"Corsica"* and landed at Sault Saint Marie Michigan on 25th September 1913. From there he moved to Ontario and finally settled in Portland Maine USA. He married Katherine Louise ? and they lived at 46 Rosedale, Portland. We visited the area a few years ago and found their house and neighbours whose mother remembered them well. They told us where they were buried and we searched a large cemetery on a very warm day but did find the grave. Horace had died in 1972 soon after losing his wife in 1971. There were a couple of surprises – we had always had cards and letters from Horace and Louise – then we found that her first name was Katherine. The second surprise was that as well as the headstone there was a plaque recording his military service as an engineer in the US Army in WW1. His career, we thought, had been spent entirely in the US Postal service - obviously not.

We took photos of the house, headstone, and plaque.

Horace Sparkes Knowles daughter Laura Christina Lavinia died at 62 High Street Milton in 1918 at the age of 25. It was a year when there was a lethal flu epidemic which killed many people towards the end of WW1. She is buried in Milton Churchyard in a family grave with her mother, stepmother (Horace's third wife) and Horace.

Horace's second marriage was to Matilda Jane McKenzie nee Webster at the Congregational Church Rainham, Kent on 8th. January 1896. Matilda was born in 1870 in Aberdeen and had been widowed after less than two years of marriage. Before starting serious family research, I had wondered how they had met given that she was born in Scotland and Horace lived in Kent. Her first husband had been working with the Royal Navy and they had come to Chatham Dockyard for his work.

Prior to their marriage Matilda stayed with Horace's sister Margaret and her husband Harry – hence the marriage in Rainham not Milton Regis.

Horace and Matilda had five children. Edward William born 1896: Dorothy born and died 1989: Gladys born 1899; Douglas born Christmas Day 1900: and Stuart born 1902. Douglas and Stuart being Scottish names, but not those of Matilda's ancestors.

In the 1901 Census the family were living at 56-60 High Street Milton Regis, also Nathanial Webster aged 22, Matilda's brother, is listed as a baker. Whether he was just visiting at the time of the Census or had come to live in Milton I am not sure, but by this time both their parents had died so maybe he had decided to leave Scotland and join his sister and her family in Kent. He married a local girl, Caroline Chopping, in 1910 and eventually died in Croydon in 1967.

From letters and post cards that I have it is obvious that Matilda did not enjoy good health. There is reference in a letter written by John Wildish Knowles to his grandson (already previously mentioned in that section) saying that he hopes that Mrs. Horace's health will improve now that they have moved to a nice house in the country. The house is called Chestnut House at Chestnut Street, on the way from Sittingbourne to Newington. The house is still there but is now two dwellings – but still has the quaint country house look complete with roses around the door.

The post cards from Matilda staying at Worthing with a cousin on her mother's side of the family – Eliza – known to the children as Auntie Lilie – say she is missing them and will be home soon. (Matilda's mother was Caroline Tidy from a family in Cowfold Sussex. She had been in service in London and probably met her husband William Webster whilst in Scotland for the shooting season with her employers. They married in a church in Covent Garden – probably arranged by her employers – then settled in Aberdeen where William was a Master Baker).

Other letters written by Matilda to a cousin also tell of how good her housekeeper is with the children – so clearly she was ill for some time before her death at the age of 36 in 1906.

Matilda was buried at the Congregational Church in Milton Regis. The church fell into a very poor state in the 1970/80s and eventually it was sold for demolition and redevelopment of the site. A local company of Funeral Directors stepped in to stop the council clearing the grave yard and did the work themselves. Remains were reinterred at the main cemetery in Sittingbourne with a memorial plaque.

Horace was now 36 years old, twice a widower and had six children with ages ranging from 4 to 16 years old.

He moved back to the High Street premises and had a house keeper and a servant to care for the family.

This must have been a difficult period of his life because in addition to the loss of his wife and the children to care for, he was running the PO, fruiterers, bakery, and grocers' businesses with his father. Edward did not retire entirely until about 1912.

The other serious problem at the time (1908) was with his youngest child Stuart, my father. He had a bone problem, not sure what, in one foot. This required treatment and surgery at Great Ormond Street Hospital in London.

I have a series of post cards of the 1908 Franco-British Exhibition in London. The exhibition was to celebrate the Entente Cordial and was visited by 8 million people. The cards depict all the different areas and buildings of the exhibition which covered 140 acres near Shepherd's Bush. All the buildings, no matter where in the world they represented – British, European or Oriental were painted white – hence the area today is known as White City.

Horace bought these cards whilst visiting his son and took them home for the other children to write to their brother.

The messages and handwriting make for poignant reading – all hoping he is getting better, some telling him about school and asking him to come home soon. One that Horace wrote to his son tells him to let the Sister know that he will bring more eggs on his next visit.

Another card to Stuart is from his grandfather Edward and Auntie – by this time Edward's first wife had died and he had married her sister 3 years later – hence auntie not grandmother. They tell him that his aunt and uncle have visited from Scotland and were sorry not to have seen him. That was followed by a card from Uncle Jack.

It must have also been quite an expense for the family. Horace would have travelled by train to London, and this was prior to the existence of the NHS so treatment I assume had to be funded by patients or their families.

I have photos of the children with Horace at this time and the children with Auntie Lilie. Stuart is sitting on his father's knee and wearing a leg brace and Edward is wearing a black arm band. One photo is of Stuart on a pony with Douglas holding the reins, taken at the Knowles' orchards – long since built on of course.

Other post cards from the same era are from the children at Worthing to their father – enjoying the pony and trap rides with Auntie Lilie – perhaps a holiday there some time after their mother died.

Two are from *"Nursie"* to her little chicks sent from Looe.

In 1909 Horace remarried – her name was Ellen Nellie Saunders, born 1875. They were married in Wigan Lancs. I have not been able to find out how or where they met, but once again the post cards sort of tell a story.

A man called George James sent a card to Horace asking if Horace junior could stay with him one more day so that they could go to the "great polo match with Wigan and Hyde Seal". The card was posted in Southport but as the stamp has been removed there is no date. Another card addressed to Stuart at PO Milton has no message but was posted in Wigan.

A best guess would be that Horace knew George James, maybe through business, and Horace junior was obviously visiting with him – maybe Horace met Ellen that way – another maybe?

From Ancestry records I have traced Ellen's parents – George and Ruth Saunders and George's occupation was a fish and fruit merchant originally from London. Another possible connection through trade?

Ellen died within one year of marrying Horace and moving to Kent. She is buried in Milton Churchyard as stated in the section on Horace's daughter Laura.

At 39 years old Horace had been widowed three times and at the 1911 census was at 62 High Street Milton Regis with his six children and a housekeeper and servant.

Horace was active in the local community as well as being the SPM and running the shops after Edward retired.

Interestingly there were 8 collections of post per day from the PO and 4 deliveries – no wonder I have post cards from Edward junior from his shop in Orpington to Horace telling him that he would be down later that evening!

Horace was a bailiff of the Ancient Manor of Milton Regis, formally a demesne held by Edward the Confessor, a Deacon of the Congregational Church, a Chairman of Milton Regis Town Council, a member of the Milton Regis Tribunal and a School Board Officer.

It was Horace and Charles that were granted probate on Edward's estate – valued at £4162-17-3.

In 1934, with all his children grown up, Horace married Minnie M M Kennett.

I was contacted last year by a lady from Sittingbourne who got my details from the local paper after I lent them some photos for publication. She said that she was the granddaughter of Horace's second wife – actually she was the granddaughter of his fourth wife. She visited us and wanted to tell us what she knew, from her grandmother, of their marriage.

Her grandmother was born in Cranbrook and had been in a very unhappy marriage. She had one son. Horace had helped her organise and pay for a divorce. This, plus the fact that she was 20 years his junior, was no doubt a scandal in those days. The granddaughter told me that her grandmother spoke to her shortly before her death so that she heard her side of the story. Horace had been very kind and they had been very happy together for the remainder of his life.

In 1934 they left Milton Regis and went to get married in Willesden, London where they opened a greengrocery shop. They retired to Bognor Regis and lived at 11 Greencourt Drive. I have photos of me as a new born taken to see Granddad Knowles for the first time – Minnie is holding me in the garden of their home.

My sister remembers her quite well: Minnie took Jean to Trafalgar Square on VJ night to see the celebrations.

Horace died in 1948 in Bognor but was buried in Milton Regis Churchyard.

Minnie stayed in Bognor for a while then returned to Sittingbourne where she lived with her son and family. She died in 1970.

When Horace left Milton Regis the sons did not want to take over the shops so they were sold, but Douglas took over the PO in 1934 and moved to premises across the High Street, he retired in 1970 when Diane Bedelle nee Knowles and her husband took over.

The Knowles family, or dynasty as it was referred to in one publication, had run the PO in Milton Regis from 1865 – 1970 and onward with Diane and Jim Bedelle.

Horace And Matilda's children; Edward William Knowles

In 1896 Horace and Matilda's first son was born. I have not been able to find out very much about Edward. He ran a greengrocer's shop in Orpington, and I have a post card date stamped 29 May 1914 telling Stuart that he would be home tomorrow and that the picture on the front was his shop.

He was in the Merchant Navy from 1921-1941 according to CLDS military lists. He married but I cannot trace a certificate. His son was also called Edward and he too went into the Navy. I understand from my sister that the son had a serious drink problem and died young.

I do remember Uncle Eddy visiting us once soon after we moved from London to Herne Bay and he attended my sister's wedding. I have a religious story book that bears the inscription on the front fly-leaf *"To Eddie Knowles from his Mam with love 1903"*.

Edward died in 1960 at Worthing.

Dorothy

Horace and Matilda's second child was a daughter, Dorothy, born and died in 1898.

Gladys

Horace and Matilda's third child was Gladys born 1899. Gladys married Herbert Frank Williams (born 1898 in Canterbury), in 1923. Herbert worked for the Post Office. Herbert died in 1957 in Chichester and Gladys died in 1968 in Sussex.

They had a son Herbert Lewis Knowles Williams born 1926. He married Sylvia Card in 1948 they did not have children. Herbert was always known as Boy – he was in the Police Service for 20+ years, then he and Sylvia bought a PO near Tonbridge, Kent. Boy died in 1999.

Douglas

Horace and Matilda's fourth child was Douglas – a Scottish name – born Christmas Day 1900. By the time of the 1901 Census Horace and Matilda had a family of 5 children and were living at 56-60 High Street Milton above the family shops.

Douglas married Doris Jenny Dodd in 1926. They did not have children.

Doris was from a local family, father James Dodd mother Ada Sidders, and had gone to school with the Knowles children. To digress for a moment to her family – her sister Mildred worked in the PO with Uncle Doug and lived to be 101 years old: her sister Bess was widowed young and bought up her son John Hallums on her own – she was the local librarian at Milton and popped across the road every morning at 11am to collect her pot of coffee from her sister at the PO!: John married but did not have a family: her brother James and his wife Winnie lived just along the road from the PO opposite the Old Court Hall, they did not have children either: her sister Alice and husband Sid lived in Bell Road Sittingbourne and had a son Graham who did not marry. An example how a large family dies out in a generation.

Doris worked a Ridham Dock in WW1 – we have a photo of the military and civilian work force plus her autograph book with many wonderful sketches done by her Ridham Dock colleagues and entries with many familiar Knowles names also. I have her engagement ring and a pretty silver locket with two very faded photos of her and Uncle Doug at the time of their engagement. She also gave me, when I was still quite a young child, her gold cross and chain – again a gift from Uncle Doug.

To return to Uncle Doug – he took over the PO from his father Horace in 1934.

The PO was moved across the High Street to number 77. The High House, as it is known, was built in the reign of James 1 originally for a Silk Merchant. It has wonderful features – the oriel window, leaded lights and ornamental panelling. Inside there is not one straight floor or ceiling, two spiral staircases and an Inglenook fireplace. He rented the righthand side of the double premises to Minnie Young who traded as a Spirella advisor. (The ladies of Milton could buy a stamp then pop next door to get measured for corsets and brassieres!)

He was Chairman of Sittingbourne Urban District Council in 1952 and read the proclamation of the accession of Queen Elizabeth the Second on the steps of Sittingbourne Town Hall.

He was President of the Milton Regis Bowling Club and had been a member since he was 18 until the time of his death in 1989. The club is one of the oldest in the country, allegedly once visited by Sir Francis Drake.

In his twenties he was in the Milton Fire Brigade when the pumps were stationed in a purpose built shed just down the hill from the High Street. Sadly, that area now looks really neglected.

He was on the Local Education Committee and regularly chaired the Appointment of Head Teachers Panel.

He also joined the Conservative club in his late teens and enjoyed a game of billiards.

I have a scrap book, made up for him by a journalist, of every newspaper article that involved him during his time as Chairman of the Council – baby shows to football matches, official functions – including one with his cousin Harry Knowles Mayor of Faversham – to some serious stuff in the council chambers.

He helped to get the Old Court Hall renovation underway and contributed some items. The last time that I visited Milton the Court Hall was open as a museum at certain times.

He was very good a preserving a bit of family as well as Milton history. I have inherited the original post horn used at Milton, a warming pan and a grandfather clock that had previously belonged to my great grandfather Edward. Two walking canes that have silver ends to their grips with initials on and a brass crib board and ash tray that were made at Milton forge, then owned by the Littlewood family. The latter was made for my father.

Uncle Doug was also quite sentimental fortunately. He gave me a silk tartan scarf and Scottish thistle brooch that had belonged to his mother, my grandmother, along with a twelve-setting tea service that had been hers and well used by the family. Also, her picnic fruit knife in a little leather case and some letters and cards that she had written to family and her children when she was convalescing in Worthing. I have her oak writing desk which Uncle Doug used in the PO for many years, complete with black and red inkpots and sealing wax.

Horace gave each of his children a silver teapot, hot water jug, milk jug and sugar basin set when they got married. This also sits and our cabinet and gets used sometimes. The traditional silver cigarette box and watch and chain gifts from father to son had been lovingly cared for – the watch and chain we lent to our son-in-law on his wedding day – my husband had his own father's.

I have been very lucky to get so much tangible family memorabilia.

The other huge debt I owe to Uncle Doug is the training I received at Milton PO which enabled me to get a good job at Canterbury PO after he retired, then a promotion to British Telecoms, at that time still part of the PO corporation, and finally, with my husband, to run our own offices at Minnis Bay and Sea Street over a nearly thirty year period.

Douglas and Doris retired to a bungalow that they had built near the Gore Court Arms Sittingbourne. I am told that that particular area is in the parish of Milton Regis. After Doris died in 1982 he was lucky enough to have an old friend who encouraged him to go on holiday – something previously unheard of except the occasional trip to Bournemouth. He announced to my horror that they were going on a boating holiday – P and O would not have been amused at the description. Three cruises later plus a couple of European trips he decided enough was enough!

He became unwell in 1987 and spent some time in hospital and with us at Sea Street Post Office. He eventually settled in a retirement home in Herne Bay and the sale of the bungalow was completed just about one week before he unexpectedly died in October 1989 in Canterbury Hospital.

Stuart

Horace and Matilda's fifth child was my father Stuart born 1902 – another Scottish name. He and Uncle Doug were quite close growing up and I believe and it was my father who seemed to lead them both into trouble sometimes! As previously mentioned he spent some time as a child in Great Ormond Street Hospital London.

He married Edna Vera Hunt in 1929 and their daughter Mary Jean Knowles was born in September 1930. Edna died in childbirth.

Stuart married again in 1934 to my mother Florence Webster born in London in 1907. She was the daughter of John Gordon Webster and Florence Salmon.

To digress again for a moment, the Salmon family lived opposite a park in Bethnal Green. My sister remembers it quite well and the house and park are still there. They were quite a talented family. Florence Salmon's brother Richard was a master carpenter and furniture maker and one of her sisters, Sarah, drew a large pen and ink drawing of the North and South American continents, complete with coastal contour lines, mountains, regions, and towns named. The bottom corner bears the inscription *"Sarah Salmon, 23 April 1878 aged 13"*. We also have two pieces of her needlework, one a sampler with hem, tucks, tabs, folds and a button hole. The other a piece of webbing with the alphabet embroidered on to it. I think these were probably a needle work test at school. Sadly, Sarah died in 1889.

Back to Stuart and Florence.

Florence moved to Milton Regis after their marriage in London and they shared Orchard House, North Street Milton with Douglas and Doris.

Stuart and Douglas carried on the family businesses after Horace and Minnie left Milton to get married until decisions were made and sales agreed.

The house is still there and according to my sister much changed from when they lived there – no front garden with wall and iron railings, no orchards out the back and surrounded by other dwellings.

I was recently contacted by a lady who gave me photos of the house soon after it was built. Her grandfather was the builder.

When war was declared in 1939 they moved back to London to help with the Webster family businesses there as man power was in short supply. John Gordon Webster, my mother's father, was a Master Baker and owned two shops, one in Elgin Avenue Maida Vale, the other in Queenstown Road Battersea. The Elgin Avenue premises were very large and had a bake house underneath where the huge ovens went out under the road. It was also an excellent air-raid shelter.

They had government contracts to supply several shelters and other sites with bread. I believe that because of this, rationing was not a problem. I think they were one of many businesses which actually prospered throughout those years.

My father was also a Special Constable and saw some horrific scenes. He had the dreadful task of identifying my mother's uncle after the bombing of Moorfield's Eye hospital where he had been a patient. (Richard Salmon, previously mentioned).

They stayed in London after the war ended and I was born in Highgate the following year. I think those post war years were again good business years and they enjoyed the London life as it slowly recovered after the dreadful 1939-1945 period.

Granddad Webster and Stuart were members of the Masonic Westbourne Grove Lodge, and my grandmother Webster was a Governor of the Royal Masonic Hospital. As well as her brooch of office in its jeweller's case, I have a badge that bears the inscription Royal Masonic Inst. For Girls 1919. It is a silver, star shaped piece with an enamelled decorated centre. Wikipedia tells me it is a steward's badge awarded for charitable work or donation.

My grandparents bought a bungalow in Herne Bay for weekend use, but after my grandfather died in 1953 it was decided to sell the shops and move to Herne Bay. My father then reverted to the family trade of Greengrocery in Sea Street plus they bought some land beside the bungalow. After an early retirement from that trade my father decided to have a change of course – they took the Rose Inn Herne Bay. Three years later my father died. My mother continued at the pub for another 12 years quite successfully – it was a bit unusual then to have a Landlady as opposed to a Landlord.

She died in 1999 aged 91.

Stuart and Edna's daughter Mary Jean Knowles – prefers to be called Jean – married Roy Alec Sinclair in 1959. Roy was in the Royal Navy and was part of the North Atlantic convoys that kept supplies moving to Russia during WW11. He was awarded the Artic Star and quite recently the Russian equivalent given in appreciation by Putin's government to all surviving veterans. They have two sons, Andrew Stuart McDonald Sinclair, and Gordon Alec Sinclair. Both are married – Andrew to Ruth Lilley and Gordon to Karen Thurlow. Andrew's sons are Sam and Thomas, Gordon's sons are Scott and Arran.

Roy died in 2017 at the age of 98.

Jean joined the Women's Land Army just before her 18th. Birthday in 1948. She was billeted at North Creek in Norfolk in a building that is now a bespoke kitchen business.

The girls worked on the farms of the landed gentry of the area harvesting root vegetables amongst other jobs. When the Land Army was disbanded she and a few other girls went to work at a nursery in Carlshalton Surrey. She returned to the family home in London in 1951.

I was born in Highgate London in 1946 and can remember quite well the Elgin Avenue shop where we lived. It was a nice part of London to live in, large houses with a flight of steps to the front doors and close to Little Venice. My first school was in Notting Hill Gate, not a good journey on a peasouper morning sometimes! I remember weekends on Hayling Island at our doctor's house. He was ET Wright, a relative of Clarissa of TV cook fame.

We drove out to Ham Common on Sundays sometimes and I also remember our journeys to Herne Bay – no Motorways, and the Rochester way sometimes at a standstill!

I went to school in Faversham – William Gibbs Grammar school for girls as it was then. My first job was at Customs and Excise HQ in London, almost next to the Tower of London. After three years there I went to work for the Guinness family bank, Guinness Mahon, in Gracechurch Street A great experience, especially the annual cocktail party at the Savoy Hotel's River Room!

I finally took up Uncle Doug's offer to go and work at Milton PO and I was there for 4 years until he retired.

Work at Canterbury PO and BT followed – which enabled me to do a bit of travelling. Two trips to California to friends of my father, Elsie and Bill Emmens, who had emigrated there in the 1920s, bought land for orange groves but had discovered oil instead! They had both attended Milton Regis school with the Knowles children.

I married James Henry Clowes in 1974 and we have a daughter Katherine Sarah.

As a family, we have travelled to the States several times to the daughter and son of the old Miltonians. Their daughter Joan and her husband live near San Francisco, and their son William lives on Orcas Island off the coast near Seattle. William and Sylvia, his wife, came over from the San Juan Islands for our daughter Katherine's wedding.

They have not just been long term, if long distant, friends but wonderful trip organisers and travelling companions.

The Milton links through family and friends in the USA and Canada is still very much alive and well.

When we married Jim was a central heating engineer working on the KCC contract throughout Kent. When the company lost the contract in 1978 Jim decided he would like to change career paths entirely and become self-employed in some sort of retail. I was totally opposed to the idea – all that responsibility 24/7 – have seen it – happy at BT. I laid some ground rules that included good area, good accommodation, something with PO, plenty of chimney pots around but not city centre. We started researching and contacted some agents who were not very encouraging. We were a bit young, not enough equity in our present house etc. etc. I spoke to the SPM at Sea Street Herne Bay as he was Federation President at the time and I had known him from when my parents had the greengrocers in Sea Street. That was in early January 1978. Later that month he called us to tell us that Minnis Bay PO would soon be on the market. On the 4th May 1978, our fourth wedding anniversary, we moved into Minnis Bay PO, I have to say on a wing and a prayer. The agents were right we couldn't really afford it!

However, within the first year our Saturday shop takings were equal to our predecessor's weekly takings and the PO salary had increased by 1k per year!

I think without knowing it we had followed Knowles and Webster family business formula – give the customers what they want – including a bit of banter. Jim was heard more than once asking a pensioner what they had done with the money he gave them last week! The answer sometimes was *"spent most of it in your shop"*.

We had six happy, but very hard- working years at Minnis, and Katherine was born there – that increased the sale of New Baby cards! Customers even sent the local vicar to see us to arrange the Christening so that it could be at the church opposite our shop during normal Sunday morning service – what about the Sunday Papers!

The SPM from Sea Street came to see us early in 1984. I remember seeing him walk into the shop and thinking that I had an idea what he wanted. He wanted to retire and was giving us first option to buy - absolutely I said. Jim was too busy in the PO to talk to him so after he left I wrote on a piece of paper "*have just agreed to buy Sea Street PO*" – and put it on the counter by Jim. I think he said *"ok!"*

In October 1984 we moved to Sea Street and were there 22 years. It was of course a much easier PO to manage. No food, no newspapers just a very busy 3 position office with three staff and us. It had been purpose built as part of a good four bed roomed family home with garden. Our years there were quite eventful business wise. I took issue with PO HQ over anything I didn't agree with, especially if it affected our office directly. As fifth generation PO owners, I felt entitled to give them the benefit of my thoughts! It paid dividends in many ways. We were asked to be part of various consultations and focus groups in London, which Jim delegated me to attend, and had numerous visits from directors and managers on fact finding missions. We always ensured that they spent a while customer facing – it did them the world of good!

We were used as a proto type experiment twice when the PO introduced new logos, colour schemes and security systems – so at least we got them to spend quite a bit of money on us!

Less happy experiences were two attempted armed hold-ups within eight months of each other, but they went away empty handed and no one harmed.

It was a happy household too, lots of extended family Christmases and celebrations. Someone once said it was so nice to have everyone under one roof. Jim's response was *"yes – but it's always my roof they're under"*.

We sold the business in 2007 and moved to Reeds Close Herne Bay partly to be near to Jim's dad who was by that time on his own at the house that he and his wife had had built in 1962. Jim's dad died in 2009 and we decided to sell our Reeds Close house and move into, what had been, Jim's family home before our marriage. We camped out with minimum furniture and builders working around us for nearly four months whilst modernisation and extensions happened.

I am afraid I cannot say that I followed the traditional Knowles service to the community to the extent of previous generations. I did however become a parent governor at a local primary school, and soon found myself chairman of finance. Then somehow allowed myself to become temporary Chairman part way through my predecessor's term of office. That temporary post lasted 18 years!

Our daughter Katherine married Simon Coish in 2012 at St. Augustine's at Westgate, just down the road from the school she attended – the Ursuline Convent.

Both Katherine and Simon changed their names by deed pole after marriage to include Clowes. She is now Katherine Sarah Clowes Coish.

Charles Knowles

Charles was the youngest son of Edward Knowles and Mary Ann Wiles, born in Milton Regis in 1871.

In the 1881 Census he is living at 56-60 High Street Milton Regis aged 9.

In the Book of Marriages Kincardineshire there is a record of Charles Knowles's marriage in 1890 to Jessie Simpson who was born in 1870 in Elgin Morayshire.

In the 1891 Census Charles and Jessie are living at 8 Victoria Road Kincardineshire and have a son Edward who was 2 months old. Edward was born 2nd. February 1891. Charles's occupation is a fruiterer, born in Milton Regis.

In the 1901 Census the family are living at 419 Great Western Road, St. Macher, Aberdeen. In addition to Charles, aged 29, and Jessie aged 29 there are four children. Edward born 1891 in Nigg, Kincardineshire: Frances born 1892: Mary Ann born 1896: and Charles R. Born 1900 – all born in Aberdeen.

Also entered on that Census return are Edward Knowles aged 65, father and visitor: Mary Ann Knowles aged 63 mother and visitor: Jeannie Simpson aged 27 sister-in-law to head of household and wife's companion. Charles's occupation was a fruit merchant.

Charles became a very successful businessman, a larger than life character who drove around in a Rolls Royce.

He started a wholesale greengrocery business in 1929 and, also acquired a lot of land. Some of the land was in the Great Western Road near where the family lived, and some north towards Deeside and Springfield Road. He had a second house at Riverton.

At the height of his career he owned seven shops. One of his main crops was daffodils. Because daffodils bloom later in Scotland than in England he exported them not only to England but also to Europe.

In the 1900s he had a market stall in Aberdeen market, and I am told that the poster is still on the wall of Knowles Fruit Services office even though the company is no longer owned by the family.

I understand that Charles and family did visit Milton Regis sometimes, driving down in his Rolls Royce!

Well after retirement age Charles apparently had issues with the tax man. He sold his businesses to a millionaire, Donald Stewart. As such negotiations would have been conducted behind closed doors little is known of the problems or the resolution.

The business is now called Knowles Fruit Services and operates from Aberdeen. Their web site states that it was founded in 1886 by Mr. Charles Knowles a fruit grower with orchards in Kent and Dublin. I am grateful to the current owner for giving me much of the information recorded here.

We were in Edinburgh in 2011 and saw an advert in the local tourist magazine for Knowes (yes, no L) farm shop tatties, washed or dirty Epicure waxy - all at their Farm Shop stall at a Farmer's market - not sure if there is a connection.

I have not been able to trace what became of Charles and Jessie's four children except the younger son may have owned a driving school.

Bernice Harriet Knowles

Bernice was the youngest child of Edward Knowles and Mary Ann Wiles born 1875.

On the 1891 Census she was living at 56-60 High Street Milton Regis and is a PO assistant to her SPM father.

In 1899 she married Andrew Willson who was born in Scotland and was then living with his parents, William Willson and Elizabeth Ryce (both born in Scotland) in Wallington Surrey. His father was a mechanical engineer, and Andrew followed his father into that trade. The wedding photo taken in the rear garden of the bride's father's house "Blenheim" London Road Sittingbourne, shows all of Edward's family and their spouses, bridesmaids etc.

The 1901 Census shows them living at *"Blenheim"* with Bernice's sister Mary Ann Knowles aged 38, and their first child, Mary Ann Willson aged four months. Their baby was born in Plumstead London.

They were staying at Blenheim whilst her parents Edward and Mary were visiting their son Charles and his family in Scotland.

By the time of the Ireland 1911 Census dated 2nd. April 1911, the family are in Belfast. Andrew is 35 and a Wholesale Fruit Merchant: Bernice is 35: Mary 10: William 8: and Christine 6. They were living at 40 Willowbank Street, Clifton, Belfast Urban no. 2 Antrim. It is stated that they can all read and write and their religion is Congregational Church.

It seems that Andrew and Bernadette were sent to Belfast as another expansion for Edward's business – presumably Andrew did not object to giving up his engineering work?

Once again, I have not been able to trace the three children further, mostly because their Christian names and surname are not uncommon. For example, if you search marriages in Ireland for Mary, William or Christine Willson there are many possibilities. That is assuming they stayed in Ireland. I have found no death record for Andrew or Bernadette in Ireland and I did attempt to look at the Clifton Cemetery records – without success.

However, a new discovery was a second marriage for Bernice. In 1926 a Bernice H Willson married a Harry Gardiner in Milton Regis. I think that given the matching names and middle initial the probability is it is the same Bernice – too much of a coincident not to be? A death of Bernice H Gardiner aged 70 is recorded in 1945 in Dover and has an attached Probate record.

It could be that Andrew died in Ireland and the family came home – but unfortunately I have found no proof of that either way.

Muriel Rooney Dell
(nee Couchman)
1927 - 2006

Written in 1999

My Name: Muriel Rooney Dell (Nee Couchman)
44 Cobblers Bridge Road
Herne Bay, Kent
CT6 8NT

Born: 13/3/1927 at 55 Lynton Road South, Gravesend, Kent

Mother: Annie Couchman (Nee Knowles)
Born: 16/5/1897
Died: 16/6/1984
Faversham

Father: Leslie Clarence Couchman
Born: 24/5/1896
Died: 1961
Faversham

My grandparents: Mr & Mrs Edward Knowles
79 Preston Street, Faversham

Mr & Mrs Couchman – Forbes Road, Faversham.

I did for a short while live in Tufton Road, Rainham, then Grandma moved back to Althestan Road, Faversham.

As much history as I know.

My mother had four brothers.

Charles (Known as Charlie).

Harry.

Jack, sometimes called John – not sure which was his correct name.

Alan (born in London, different mother, raised as one of the family).

Do not know who was eldest.

Norman died young.

Ciss unmarried – Edward.

Uncle Char as I know him, married now correct name am not at all sure she was known to everyone as Cis, but I think her name could have been Harriet (Horton). Her maiden name I have no knowledge of. They did for a while live over Whitstable shop until they went up to 'Jaffa', Canterbury Road, a lovely house in its own plot, had storage sheds at bottom of the garden, which backed onto the railway line, (I had some lovely holidays there). They had three children. Gordon, Eric, Hazel (Uncle Char and auntie Cis' ashes scattered at cricket ground, Whitstable).

Gordon was up to two years ago still alive, living at Tankerton. His wife's name was Phyllis, she passed away a few years ago. They had one son, Ivan, he and his Dad were photographed together in the local paper some 2-3 years ago. Ivan if my memory is correct did marry and I think has sons – but his wife's name no idea or where they live now. (Ivan married Yvonne Edwards of HB (Ron Edwards sister I believe, they have two sons, Gary and Paul).

*Since doing the start of history, Gordon has passed away. Died at Queen Victoria Hospital, Herne Bay, October, 14th 1999 aged 85.

Eric. His first wife's was Sheila (maiden name don't remember), they lived in Cromweel Road, Whitstable, as you walked up to station the house was on the left. They had two sons – probably three, their eldest was Michael. I last saw him when he was about 18 months two years ago and according to my cousin in Faversham from my Dad's side the family Michael has the health food shops – probably now run by one of his sons.

Eric's second wife, no details only that they ran the '3 K's' amusements in Sheereness. Not sure, but I think Eric is still alive.

Hazel. Worked in the family greengrocery shop etc in 1940, married Mervyn Tutt in fact married from my Mum's Dad's house in Gravesend (I have a photo my Dad took of Hazel in our back garden on her wedding day). Mervyn was a Whitstable chap, but when called up came strangely to Milton Army Barracks - Gravesend (now gone) and he came to our home whenever he wasn't on duty. Merv went to France soon after they married, was captured not long after and spent until peace declared in a P.O.W camp XXB – East Prussia.

After his return home he and Hazel ran a successful fruit and veg shop in High Street, Margate and had a flat opposite side of the road, unfortunately to their sorrow never had a family. They took early retirement and had a bungalow 'Dream Ours' if I remember correctly in Northumberland Avenue, Margate. But Mervs health was of great concern. They didn't want to be parted again and committed suicide in their car (my brother knows more about this).

Harry. Married Nellie, cannot remember her maiden name, she had a sister Dorrie, or so she was called - she and Nellie came from Davington and in years to come I think Dorrie made her home with Harry & Nellie. Harry & Nellie lived in Stone Street, Faversham in a three story house, it was the last house I think along passed Cottage Hospital on that side. Then they moved into the premises of 79 Preston Street after Grandma Knowles died. Harry was Mayor of Faversham twice. They had two sons and two daughters.

Harry Jnr - son of Harry (Young Harry as he was known, he did marry, but I don't know her name). I believe they parted, do not know if Harry is still alive.

Colin married a nurse, but don't know her name or where they lived or if they had any family or if still alive.

Mary did work at the theatre in Canterbury, she did marry, had two children - possibly a third and lived in a very old beamed house in Ospringe. Do not know if she is still alive.

Prudence. I last saw her at my wedding in November 1947 and have no idea where she is.

Alan - youngest brother of my mother. Married Sybil (cannot remember her maiden name), they lived in St Martins Road, Canterbury, after the bombing moved to the mall, Faversham. They did not have a family but adopted a daughter named Christine, she did marry but where she is now I have no idea. Alan and Sybil parted.

Jack or John (not sure which was his real name). He worked with his father until he got his own place. He married May, cannot remember her maiden name or whether she came from Faversham area. They had a shop in high street, Chatham and in later years lived on the premises, previously lived up Maidstone Road, Chatham. They had a large family, have written names I remember, but not in the order they were born.

Rufus - I believe he did at one time work in H.M. Prison service and did marry.

Norman - Worked for ABC Cinemas, was manager at Gravesend at 'The Super', then across the road at 'The Regal', then down into Kings Street to the then 'Majestic', from there he went to the Dover area I believe, he returned to live in the Gillingham area - do not know if still alive. He married twice, his first wife was Marjorie, they had one son (name escapes me at present), Marjorie had a fall from a ladder picking cherries and was paralysed for the rest of her life, at first was taken to Barts (St Bartholomew's), Rochester and then to Papworth where she died. Have no name for his second wife, but they had several children.

Teddy - real name Edward, died aged about 11, and is buried in Faversham cemetery, his grave bears a statue of an Angel.

Ray - He I know did RAF service and I think in time married, but died years ago.

Rene - She was the eldest daughter – and did marry I know and was at one time manageress of a toy shop in Chatham. No idea where she is now – but I believe still in the Medway area.

Jacqueline - Have no idea where she is now.

Dawn - Have no idea where she is now.

Alec's on tree, name does come to mind now.

I know my mothers brother Alan was the youngest, but who was eldest out of her other brothers cannot recall now. One of her brothers was in the army during the first world war so my mother travelled six days a week from Faversham to Dover by train leaving home early and getting home late, as she had to take charge of the family Dover shop – remembered the shells falling.

Annie Knowles married Leslie Clarence Couchman at Faversham Congregational Church, Gravesend - James was then a regular in the Royal Navy, Stoker Petty Officer and served for some years to come.

Daughter Ruth born 28th March 1949 (twice married) two sons.

Son David born 30th September 1950, two girls and one son.

Son James born 3rd November 1956, divorced, no family.

Daughter Yvonne born 4th September 1958, married two girls.

My brother John Leslie was born 19th June 1935, worked for Midland Bank – being retired some time lives on edges of Broadstairs. Married Dorothy Kennett – Sittingbourne, had daughter Christine & son Michael.

My sister Louie Ann was born 20th November 1936 (worked in offices of J.E. Hall, Dartford, then A.P.C.M Northfleet) married George Marven on November 1958 had one daughter Alison, son Christopher, son Richard, son Graham. My sister & her husband now live in Bengeo, Hertfordshire.

Our father was an engineer did his apprenticeships at Chatham Dockyard, then went to work for A.P.C.M (Blue Circle) 'Kent Works' Stone Crossing, Dartford, Kent. Now demolished. He did for a long while cycle to work (shift work until late 1940s). He saw a terrible accident on Stonebridge Hill (Cobbled Street) Northfleet from then onwards on the train.

Dad came from a large family - one niece Vera is still alive and living in St Mary's Road, Faversham. No knowledge of any others still alive.

From Bygone Kent book can find lots of Knowles history also other books, see last page.

Grandfather Knowles, must have had brothers and sisters - as their were Knowles's in Ireland & Scotland and Buckinghamshire.

I can remember going to visit aunt Polly (would have been my great aunt) at Chalkwell Road, Milton, Sittingbourne. You went under the railway bridge - to me then always seemed a huge house, aunt Polly was bedridden, but did beautiful fine, lace (I've got a tablecloth with edging she made, it was given to my mother in fact I think she had several) who gave one to me. I know my mother had cousins who ran the sittingbourne shop. We would at same time spend time with Auntie Hart (mum's Aunt), whether this was short for Harriet or her surname I have no idea, she lived in Rock (now not sure if it was road or avenue), but was in Sittingbourne, she had two daughters,

Mary (who to me was always auntie Mary, she married Bill McArthur, they lived in Canterbury and had no children - Bill Was in the printing business and went to see the works once, but they did part company and auntie Mary lived in Caversham, Berks until she died years ago now. Her sisters name was Chris (not sure if short for Christine) and not sure if there was a brother - Chris lived at Dover.

From the time I was born until Grandma Knowles died my mother took me on the M&D bus (Maidstone & District) No 26 from the then bus depo on the Overcliffe at Gravesend straight through to Faversham, took exactly two hours, we used to go home once a month on a Friday PM and came home Sunday afternoon.

Saw a horse drawn cart lose its load of mangel wurzels all over the road in front of the bus.

Long before I went to school, I knew all the names of the shops, towns, villages and used to look for special things. Large statues in a front garden just past Key Street, the Orchards. Brick works and their chimneys, hop fields, water lane, Ospringe. I knew many of the shopkeepers in Preston Street then, Jasheys sweet shops - in years to come use to go with a 1p and get a bag of chocolate drops covered with coloured pieces. Mains - watchmakers etc. Clarke's Dairy used to play with Billy Clarke, he had a lovely rocking horse and in the shop a lovely marble counter often had a lump of honeycomb on it. Clarkes was next to the building now the Fleur-de-lis centre. Then there was the pork butchers in the lane opposite No 79.

Annie Reeves and her mother – Annie was a friend of Mums, lived up in the old coach house at top of Preston Street.

Carters the newsagent. Vera Carter became Vera Gibbs and strangely enough they in time came to live in Gravesend - Vera's husband Bert (Albert) was head gardener for Gravesend council, had daughter Pauline, she taught me to swim in the the open air cold baths at Gravesend before the second world war, she keeps in touch with me. She lives in Stevenage, Hertfordshire and had twin brothers, David & Keith. David died very suddenly and a few years ago lived in Surrey. Keith lives in Essex both married Gravesend girls, Paulines husband (Ven) is from Gravesend. Bridgens the Florists just across from the town hall. Elsie Brigden was a friend of Mums.

Then across the road from Brigdens a few down was Bulgers the Butchers. Mum had a friend who worked in Faversham post office, then Canterbury but cannot remember her name. Also remember the old fire station near the market place.

The swings in the recreation ground and the footbridge over the railway from where you watched the engines go around on
the turntable.

Remember also the dark stone floored kitchen in Preston Street, with a big old black range also the outside toilet with squares of newspaper hanging on a rail.

The large storehouse bottom of yard with large platform scales, where the chaps would weigh me, also the big outside wooden staircase to other floor.

Also remember the big wooden shutters which covered the shop front (no glass all open) hearing folk bring them down the passage way side of 79 in the morning and back at closing time.

I Remember sitting in the shop on an upturned bushel basket and being given brown bags and a wooden tumbler shaped measure (different sized ones) and measuring out peanuts in their shells then. Also when older being allowed to carefully remove bunches of grapes from a large tub full of tiny pieces of cork in which the grapes were packed. Incidentally these cork pieces made a lovely filling for a pouffe.

My Mum had one for all the years I can remember, what happened to it I don't know. Also can remember the large slabs of sticky dates.

Oranges in slated tall boxes secured with wire. Cherries and soft fruit in special baskets, also plums different varieties. Tangerines displayed with every so often one wrapped in silver paper. In these days, oranges, grapefruits etc had fine paper with a name and country wrapped round them.

Hands of bananas hanging on big hooks. Apples displayed in a special shaped way. The only thing I didn't like at 79 Preston Street was when the large saucepan of 'lights' was being cooked to feed the cats.

Grandma Knowles had a maid, I suppose you would call her, what her name was I don't know, but I called her 'Fairy', why I do not know, she took me to her house one afternoon up Preston Street, into Stone Street and into Cross Lane, her father took me to see all the rabbits he had in their hutches, in time I had a wee black one, had it as a pet at Gravesend for a long while.

Also, went twice if not three times with my mother to the Faversham Almshouses at the end of Stone Street to visit Mr Mercer, he was my mothers school teacher, I remember having a cup of tea and a thick arrowroot biscuit.

I remember also hanging out a window above the shop to watch the torchlight-flares carnival. Also odd piece of family connections, uncle Char had his shop in the main street, Whitstable, his daughter named Hazel. Few doors down was another Greengrocers Harry & Gert Couchman – this Harry was one of my fathers older brothers – daughter Margaret and Margaret and Hazel both nieces of my parents were friends until Hazels death. Maragret married Ron Martin, he died quite a long time ago as far as I know Margaret lives at Tankerton, she had one daughter and one son.

Family history in books;

Portrait of a seaside town - Whtistable 1-4
Douglas West

Faversham by Peter Kennett
In old photos, Eric Swain

Bygone Kent
Volume 19 No 4

Contains a good deal of history on the Knowles family.

Edward Raymond Ian Knowles
1983 -

Written in 2017

The following information, in support of and adding to the work of William Knowles of Sheerness, comes from several sources; Faversham and North East Kent news, Faversham News, Faversham historians Peter Stevens & Arthur Percival, Chatham News, Bygone Kent Life, The Whitstable Times, The Kentish Express, 'Who Got In – a brief history of local election results from 1945 to 1972' by Reg Winton, Ministry of Defence, www.familysearch.org, www.faversham.org, www.ancestry.com, College of Arms - William George Hunt, the Library & Museum of Freemasonry, 23&Me, Company of Watermen and Lightermen, The Rochester Bridge Trust, 'Dogs of War: Sir Hugh Calveley & Sir Robert Knolles' by Tony Bostock.

Edward Knowles was born in Milton Regis, Kent, on November 7, 1860, and was the eldest son of Edward Knowles and Mary Ann Wiles. Edward was from a large family of five brothers and three sisters. Edward continued the family fruit business, 'Knowles & Son', from his father, Edward Snr, which had branches in Kent, Dublin and Aberdeen. Edward also had two *"colourful"* stints on the Faversham council. Edward died in Faversham, Kent on December 15, 1930.

Edward had two children with his first wife - married on May 2, 1884 in Milton, Kent - Alice Fanny Collard, who died aged 27 in November 1888, the children were Edward Charles Knowles born April 10, 1885 and Alice Fanny Knowles born November 9, 1888. Edward married his second wife Ann Hams on August 4, 1890 in Faversham, and they had five children together, John (Aka: Jack) born August 20, 1892, Norman born May 2, 1899, Charlie born October 30, 1893, Annie born May 16, 1896 and Harry born January 25, 1901, all of whom I will go into more detail about. Edward also had an illegitimate son with a girl that worked in his shop, the boy, named Alan, was born in 1912 and brought up in the family.

The family fruit business was operating at 77 Preston Street, Faversham, Kent and moving to 79 Preston Street in 1893, under the name 'Knowles & Son', Edward and his brothers extend the business as far as Dublin and Aberdeen. Edward had an orchard at Uplees, Faversham where he employed numerous fruit pickers. In addition to his pioneering in the sale of strawberries to Aberdeen, he also claimed to be the first grower to export English apples to Beunos Ayres.

According to Faversham historian, Peter Stevens, Edward - who always wore a bowler hat - was known for his generosity, delivering oranges to the local schools at Christmas. A Chatham & Rochester news article on my father, Norman Knowles, mentions that Edward ran a cinema in converted stables behind Preston Street, Faversham.

Edward became a councillor of Faversham in 1901, beating a Mr E Chambers in a poll with 796 votes and served a three year term, and after a lengthy exodus from local politics, returned in May 1929, less than one year before his death, beating a Mr Turner with 1,501 votes to 651. Edward campaigned for and against several local issues while on the council, including the closing of Preston Street by the Railway company in 1898, which he ordered a petition against, without success, then against the Gas Company because of the poor illuminating quality of the gas, then three years later when the electricity supply was established, Edward campaigned against anomalies in the charges.

Perhaps most well known of all, is Edward's fury about increases in water charges, by the Faversham Water Company, a photo appeared in the local paper of him pumping water at the town water pump in protest. The pump is located just behind Guildhall still to this day, although is no longer in use. Edward was know to subscribe himself as *"Your Old Friend, Knowles"* in trade announcements, which became a well-known reference to him.

Edward Charles Knowles was the first and only son of Edward's marriage to Alice Fanny Collard. He was born on April 10, 1885 at 79 Preston Street, Faversham, and married Annie Rose Reeves in 1908 at St Mary's Church, Dover, Kent. Edward died on October 23, 1911 aged 26.

Alice Fanny Knowles , also known as 'Sis', was Edward's second and last child with Alice. Alice was born on November 9, 1888 in Holborn Street, Aberdeen, Scotland and worked as a Book Keeper and Fruiterer for the family business.

Edward's first wife Alice was born May 27, 1861 and died November 13, 1888, aged 27 and only four days after giving birth to Alice. Edward and Alice had married in 1884 in Milton, Kent. I do not know the exact cause of her death, but assume it was perhaps from complications giving birth to Alice. Edward would have been 28 when she died.

John Knowles was the eldest son from Edward's marriage to Ann Hams. John, also known as 'Jack', was born at 79 Preston Street, Faversham, Kent on August 20, 1892. He married Elizabeth Mary Wilbraham at a Dover registry office in 1913. John and Elizabeth had eight children together, Rufus born February 11, 1914, Norman born October 29, 1915, Raymond born March 14, 1920, Irene born April 11, 1924, Edward born March 25, 1926, Alec born August 11, 1928, Jacqueline born September 11, 1930 and Dawn born January 5, 1938. Jack took the Knowles fruit business to Medway, where he had a shop at No351, Chatham High Street. Legend has it, he kept live pigs at the back of the shop! I know at some point John suffered bankruptcy, and later became a coal merchant. I remember my father describing him as tough, with a short temper. Again, consistent with a lot of the Knowles men, he liked a drink!

John was a Freemason of the Peace & Harmony Lodge No199 in Dover, Kent, where he was initiated on December 5, 1932, passed on March 6, 1933 and raised on April 3, 1933. He later joined Loyal & True Lodge No4050 – a shopkeeper's lodge - in Chatham, Kent, on January 19, 1944 and became Worshipful Master there in 1951. He also joined Royal Arch Chapter of Antiquity No20 in Chatham, Kent, where he was exalted on July 5, 1944. He held Provincial Rank (Kent) in 1961 as Provincial Assistant Grand Director
of Ceremonies.

Before moving to Medway, John lived with the family for a time at Rushmere Farm, the address being Throwley, Charing in Faversham. John's daughter Irene was born at the farm. My father told my siblings and I many stories about his childhood on Rushmere Farm, including the time a bull escaped from its pen and ran down the embankment and into the pond! There was also a big figure-like stain on the farmhouse window that looked like a ghost, which all of the children were afraid of. There were several horses on the farm, a favourite of my fathers was called 'Dapple Grey'.

I believe that fruit was produced on the farm for the family business. The more exotic fruit was shipped in from overseas, my father told me one story of when he was present as they took an order of bananas in wooden crates - presumably from some far flung exotic destination - and when one of the lids came off a huge spider jumped out and bit him on the leg! Thankfully his quick thinking mother, Elizabeth, sucked any potential poison from the wound.

According to one story, there were several workers that the farm employed that had accomodation issues, but John allowed them to stay on the farm as long as they voted for the Conservatives! I visited the farm in February 2014, finally finding it after taking some wrong turns down some narrow country lanes. It is still called Rushmere Farm and has horses and chickens. It is exactly as I imagined, an idyllic setting for any child.

I'm told John also owned several properties in Chatham at some stage, including one on Maidstone Road. According to the Last Will and Testament of John's wife Elizabeth – made December 19, 1973 – she was living at 26 Speedwell Avenue, Weedswood Estate, Chatham, Kent.

Elizabeth's Will also leaves land owned at Bridgewood, Bluebell Hill, Nr. Rochester to her sons Rufus and Norman, her daughters Irene, Jacqueline and Dawn, and also her daughter-in-law Kathleen, each receiving one sixth.

Charles Knowles was born October 30, 1893 in Faversham, Kent to Edward and Ann. He married Harriet Hilda Horton on June 9, 1913 and they had three children together, Gordon Charles Knowles born April 7, 1914, Eric James Knowles born November 5, 1915 and Hazel Knowles born March 7, 1920. Charles ran the family fruit business in Whitstable, Kent, operating from No39 High Street.

More is covered about Charlie in his grandson Ivan's section.

Harry Knowles was the youngest son of Edward and Ann. Harry was born in Faversham, Kent on January 25, 1901. Harry married Nellie Harris and they had four children together, Harry born August 8, 1923, Colin born 1927, Mary born 1933 and Prudence born 1942. Harry continued the family fruit business 'Knowles & Son' in Faversham, operating from 79 Preston Street. Harry was a local councilor and Mayor of Faversham in 1949-50. Harry died in Canterbury, Kent on January 9, 1975.

Harry Knowles was Mayor of Faversham in 1949-50. He enjoyed a successful political career, which extended from 1936 to 1970 and on his final retirement from the Council was made a Freeman of the Borough. At his 'freedom ceremony' he recalled the many hours he had spent on council work since the 1930s, but said there had been compensations. He had met interesting and important people including Sir Winston Churchill and Lord Montgomery.

He always stood as an Independent which was probably for the benefit of his custom and customers; best not to show any political persuasion! He was always very popular.

In 1948 Harry was made a J.P and served the Faversham bench for more than 20 years. He was one of the prime movers in re-starting the Faversham Carnival after the war and before electricity was nationalised he was Chairman of the local Electricity Committee. He also served as Chairman of the Faversham Chamber of Trade, President of Faversham Hospital Charity Cricket Competition and, for some the most important, as President of Faversham Town Football Club. He retired in 1969. He was a greengrocer with an open fronted shop in Preston Street. Sadly the Knowles shop at 79 Preston Street was demolished to be replaced by what was recently (in the 21st century) the 'Chainsaw Massacre' store. It is now an undertaker's.

The Knowles way of doing business was to advertise, and they served Faversham people for more than 80 years. Harry succeeded his father Edward Knowles in the 1930s, and in the 1940s and 1950s Harry's brother Charles ran a similar shop in Whitstable.

In his booklet (which is still available at the Fleur de Lis in Faversham) 'Who Got In – a brief history of local election results from 1945 to 1972', the late Reg Winton who served as Councillor, Mayor and Town Clerk, writes:-

"Harry Knowles, affectionately known as 'Cracknuts', was popular, speaking to everyone, especially if they bought any of his fruit and nuts from his Preston Street shop. In the 1945 Borough Council election he came second of the five elected with 1,973 votes, in 1949 second again with 2,996 votes, in 1952 he topped the poll with 2,644 votes, in 1955 top again with 2,801 votes, and in 1958 top again with 2,607 votes."

A 1938 notice in the Faversham News gave notice of a Social at the Institute, which was in East Street and stated that Councillor H Knowles will entertain during the evening. He clearly liked to socialise and in the Faversham Society photograph collection there is one taken in 1956/7 at the Willow Tap public house which was on The Brents showing Harry with fellow councillors Gordon Ely, John Jones, Lily Older, and F.G Bishop, Town Clerk , Ray Sharp, the deputy Town Clerk and Albert Fever, another official.

Like many other Knowles's, Harry was a Freemason of Athelstan Lodge No4024, in Faversham.

In March 2014, I visited Guildhall by special appointment by the Town Clerk, Jackie Westlake OBE. Guildhall is where the Faversham town council meet and is where Harry served his time as Mayor. While there I was able to take some photographs of the inside and the various photos/portraits that hang on the walls, including Harry's. It was the first time I had seen his official photograph. These photos can be seen in the photo pages of this book.

In early 2014, I had an extensive email conversation with local Faversham historians, Peter Stevens and Arthur Percival, who informed me that there are plans to name a road in Faversham after the Knowles's, who had a profound impact on local life for several generations. The road, which is in a 'bank of names' for potential future developments, may be known as 'Knowles Way', because their 'way' was to advertise. The idea was suggested by the youngest daughter of Harry Knowles, Prudence Latham in a letter dated 19th November 2009.

I also found the minutes of a Faversham Town Council meeting on www.faversham.org dated April 2, 2012, a section titled 'Approval for naming a new road – Foundry site, Oare Road' states as follows –

"Swale Borough Council has received an application to name a site off Oare Road. The old Foundry site of Seager Road, Faversham, will have an area for housing with the access from Oare Road and I enclose a copy of site plans for your use. Faversham Town Council has previously asked the Borough Council to use the names of Harry Knowles (former businessman and Mayor of Faversham) and Lilian Older (first woman Labour Councillor of Faversham) for any new road name. The Borough Council are now suggesting, therefore that these roads should be Knowles Avenue and Older Avenue, although it has been suggested to me that perhaps the name Harry Knowles Close might be more appropriate but I shall be glad of your instructions."

At the time of writing the road naming has not been made, and it is not known for sure when and if the council will ever action this.

Alan Knowles was the fifth son of Edward, and the result of a relationship he had with one of the girls that worked in one of his fruit shops. Perhaps quite scandalous really, especially when taking into account the era and his local social standing. Regardless, Ann Hams, Edward's wife, brought Alan up as one of the family. According to www.familysearch.org on the England and Wales birth registration Index, Alan was born in 1912 in London sometime between July and September. His biological mothers name was Milstead. According to notes made by Muriel Dell, Alan married a Sybil, and they lived in St Martins Road, Canterbury and after the bombing moved the The Mall, Faversham. They adopted a daughter named Christine, and at some point Alan and Sybil separated.

Annie Knowles was Edward's only daughter with Ann Hams. She was born on May 16, 1896 and married Lesley Couchman. Annie was an Assistant Fruiterer for the family business. Annie died on June 16, 1984.

Edward also had a son, **Norman Knowles**, born 1899 in Faversham who sadly died at 10 months old on March 14, 1900. My grandfather John, would have been seven years old at the time of Norman's death, such a thing would undoubtedly have a profound effect on any young child. It's almost certain that John named his second son Norman, my father, after his younger brother, something which is well documented in this book is the naming of subsequent children after deceased children within the family, which was common place.

Rufus William John Knowles was the first son of John Knowles and Elizabeth Wilbraham. Rufus was born February 11, 1914. He was a fruiterer and was in the Royal Air Force during WWII. I was told at some stage in middle age he had cancer, which he beat and recovered from. He married Margaret Thompson on September 16, 1942 and they had two sons together, John born February 18, 1945 and Patrick born March 17, 1948. Rufus outlived all of his brothers, and died sometime between 2005 and 2008, I don't know the exact date and have been unable to successfully obtain a death certificate. According to the Last Will and Testament of Rufus's mother Elizabeth, he was living at 286 Castle Road, Chatham, Kent in 1974. In later life he lived on London Road, Rainham, Kent.

I remember on one occasion meeting Rufus, when I was around 14 years old, he was partially blind so came close to my face to have a good look, then declared *"He's a Knowles!"*, whatever it is a Knowles looks like! Rufus's son John married Valerie Fuller and they had two children, Laura Ann Knowles born January 16, 1975 and Christopher Martyn Knowles born May 29, 1978.

Rufus's son Patrick married Allison Turner and they had two children, Samantha Kim Knowles born April 22, 1976 and Daniel John Knowles born October 22, 1978.

Like his father, Rufus was a Freemason of Loyal & True Lodge No4050 in Chatham, Kent. He was initiated on November 21, 1951, passed on March 19, 1952 and raised on November 19, 1952.

After my father died, my family lost contact with Rufus, but I know one of his grandsons joined the police force and one of his granddaughters became a bouncer/doorwoman. I last saw Rufus at my father's funeral in 2000.

Norman Edward Frank Knowles , my father, was the second son of John Knowles and Elizabeth Wilbraham. Norman was born on October 29, 1915 in Whitstable, Kent. He served in the RAF during WWII as an Aircrafthand and later as a Wireless Operator. He was a Cinema Manager for ABC Cinemas for almost 50 years. In 1939 he married Marjorie Eileen Smith and they had a son together, Peter, born in 1948. Norman and Marjorie separated and he later married Mary Maureen Roach, my mother, at a Dover registry office in 1975. Marjorie died in 1974. Together, Norman and Mary had seven children, Maria born January 18, 1971, Nathalie born July 21, 1972, Simon born April 2, 1976, Rebecca born September 4, 1979, Edward born April 1, 1983 and twins, James and Andrew born August 6, 1984. Norman died in Gillingham, Kent, on October 1, 2000.

Norman grew up on Rushmere Farm in Faversham, and had early aspirations to become a teacher. However, I believe for reasons mainly due to his father John's bankruptcy, he could not pursue higher education to do so. Norman and Marjorie, lived at 29 Dour Street, Dover, followed by 485 Canterbury Street, Gillingham, and later a bungalow at 34 Chicago Avenue, Gillingham.

Norman was called up for national service with the Royal Air Force and was enlisted on June 29, 1938. In 2014 I applied for his WWII service record through the Ministry of Defence. His service number was 812101, and his discharge date was December 25, 1942 on grounds of health; I believe poor hearing being the reason.

The record stated his total service as four years and 211 days. He began his service as an Aircrafthand, an entry position within the RAF, and later a Wireless Operator working with Morse code, a role that he blamed on his deteriorating hearing in later life; he wore two hearing aids.

His record lists 500 Squadron as his unit, which was based in Detling, Kent. My father was proud of his RAF Service and would talk about it from time to time. Apparently he was known as 'Fruity', because his RAF peers were aware his family were in the fruit trade! I remember a conversation when I was young concerning his entitlement to WWII service medals, which he never claimed because he 'didn't see the point'. Once I received his service record I wanted to claim the medals on his behalf, which took several months, but I was delighted to receive two medals in November 2014; the War Medal and the Defence Medal.

On Monday, March 29, 1944, Norman joined ABC Cinemas as a Trainee Manager, and was later promoted to Manager. He worked at several ABC Cinemas in the South East of England over a 50 year career, these included The Super in Gravesend, The Majestic, ABC Dover, The Ritz/ABC Chatham and relief work at Cinemas in London. At some point in the 1960s or 1970s he was made 'Championship Manager of the year', which was a well respected honour within the cinema industry. One thing to bear in mind is that this was an era when a Cinema Manager was a locally prestigious and well respected role to have, not just another job like it is probably seen today. Cinemas of Norman's era were usually grand art deco buildings placed at the heart of the high streets, and going to the cinema was an event!

Norman reluctantly retired from ABC Cinemas, at this point a company acquired by Cannon Cinemas, in 1991, aged 75 (He had officially retired in 1980). His last Cinema was the ABC in Chatham, which was the only cinema I have a memory of him at. He was well respected by the staff and they were very sad to see him leave. My Mum would take my brothers and I to the ABC Chatham regularly, and we would be allowed in for free, plus free chocolate and drinks! This continued for a few years after Norman retired, until the last of the staff that worked for him were phased out.

Norman would regularly appear in the local news in stories linked to the Cinema. Two articles I have that appeared in the Chatham News include one titled *"A great double feature"*, a story about Norman becoming a father of twins at 68, and *"When a naked seaman tried to save Pinocchio"*, an article on his retirement where he talks about an amusing memory involving a drunken cinema goer. The headline tells you the rest!

Like his father, Norman was a Freemason of Loyal & True Lodge No4050 in Chatham, Kent. He was initiated on January 16, 1946, passed on March 20, 1946 and raised on March 19, 1947.

During the 1980s, Norman was a parent governor at the Chatham Grammar School for Girls, while Maria and Nathalie were pupils.

Norman and Marjorie had one son together, Peter Norman Knowles who was born in Chatham in 1948. Marjorie was paralysed from the waist down after an accident while fruit picking and was confined to a wheelchair for the rest of her life, she had fallen from a ladder. Marjorie died in 1974. Marjorie and Norman had separated several years before her death, and Norman later married my mother, Mary, in 1975.

Norman met Mary Roche at the ABC Cinema in Gravesend, where she worked as a cashier. There was a 32 year age gap between them. They had seven children together. Mary and Norman rented a house together at 30 Salisbury Road, Dover in 1970, and then in 1981 they moved back to 34 Chicago Avenue in Gillingham. When Norman and Marjorie separated, Marjorie remained at Chicago Avenue and lived with her Mother. After Marjorie's death, her mother continued to live in the house until her death. In 1981, Norman moved back there with Mary, Maria, Nathalie, Simon and Rebecca.

By 2004, it was just myself, Andrew and my mother living at Chicago Avenue. Maria, Nathalie, Simon and Rebecca had 'flown the nest' and James was at University. The house was sold and we moved to Rainham, Kent, in December that year.

Raymond Ian Knowles was the third son of John Knowles and Elizabeth Wilbraham. He was born on March 14, 1920 in Faversham, Kent. He had a decorated eight year career in the Royal Air Force spanning all of WWII, starting as an Aircraftsman Second Class and rising to Acting Sergeant. Raymond married Kathleen Jones in 1946 in Chatham, Kent, and they had one daughter together, Jill Knowles born 1949. Raymond died on September 13, 1963.

Raymond grew up on Rushmere Farm in Faversham. Raymond was described as *"a bit of a maverick"* and liked to be where the action was, apparently he could be found regularly hanging around with the gypsies that stayed on the farm!

While I am lacking on information on Raymond's life as a whole, one thing he was well known for was his distinguished career in the RAF during WWII. My father in particular was very proud of his brother's service. In 2014 I applied for Raymond's RAF service record, his service number was 812105, his enlistment date was June 19, 1938 and his discharge date, March 3, 1946. Raymond was part of several units and squadrons, the service record I was sent notes them all as abbreviations, but the ones I know of are 500 Squadron, 248 Squadron, Air Command South

East Asia, Casualty Air Evacuation Unit and 194 Squadron. He began his career as an Aircraftsman Second Class in 1938, then Aircraftsman First Class in 1940, Leading Aircraftsman again in 1940, Corporal in 1942 and rising to Acting Sergeant in 1945.

Like his father, Raymond was a Freemason of Loyal & True Lodge No4050 in Chatham, Kent. He was initiated on September 16, 1959, passed on September 21, 1960 and raised on September 20, 1961. In Raymond's Masonic record I retrieved from The Library and Museum of Freemasonry, it states his employment at time of initiation as a Fish Merchant.

Raymond died aged 43 from carcinoma of the stomach (gastric cancer), my father believed it may have been a result of his time served in Burma during WWII, maybe from wartime emissions such as asbestos, radon or depleted uranium. It was common for veterans to become ill soon after wars because of exposure to such elements. I also acquired Raymond's death certificate, which had his profession at the time of death as 'Salesman/House Furnisher' and his address as 5, Rosemary Close, Chatham, Kent.

According to the Last Will and Testament of Raymond's mother Elizabeth, his wife Kathleen was left one sixth of land owned at Bridgewood, Bluebell Hill, Nr. Rochester in 1974.

The other children of John and Elizabeth who I have little information on include **Irene May Knowles**, born April 11, 1924 at Rushmere Farm, Faversham. She married Harry T Rogers on July 5, 1942 at St Mary's Church, Chatham, Kent, and they had one son together, also called Harry Rogers.

It was a family tree created by Harry in 2003 that was passed along to me in 2013 which first sparked my interest in researching the Knowles family history, I never met Harry as he died several years before his tree found me. His tree had been passed to my half brother Peter and it was Peter that eventually passed it to me.

Irene was a shop manager and a custodian of Temple Manor in Strood, Kent.

According to the Last Will and Testament of Irene's mother Elizabeth, she was living at 70 Chestnut Avenue, Walderslade, Chatham, Kent in 1974. Elizabeth left Irene one sixth of land owned at Bridgewood, Bluebell Hill, Nr. Rochester, two diamond brooches and a glass cabinet in her Will.

Edward Knowles born March 25, 1926 and died in 1937 at Great Ormond Street hospital in London. An obituary, printed in the Faversham News, does not specify his illness, only that he was taken ill 'about the middle of May' and passed away before he was due to have an operation. I think it was Edward who died of a brain tumor. When riding his bike one day he felt poorly so knocked at a ladies' door asking for a glass of water, and when she returned he had collapsed, or so the story goes.

Alec Knowles was born August 11, 1928 and died in 1940. I have little information on Alec, but I believe he died in a bicycle accident of some sort. It cannot have been easy for John and Elizabeth, losing two sons so young within a few years.

Jacqueline Ann Knowles was born on September 11, 1930 in Dover, Kent. She married Keith Arnold on June 16, 1953 and they had two children together, Nicholas born May 19, 1956 and Maxine born November 13, 1962. Jacqueline lives on Hollywood Lane, Rochester, Kent.

Dawn Knowles , the youngest child of John and Elizabeth, was born January 5, 1938 in Faversham, Kent. She married Alan Coster on March 30 1959 at Ebeneezer Church, Chatham, Kent. Dawn died on October 5, 1997.

Searching for a right to arms

In January 2014 I decided to try and find out if our particular Knowles family line had ever had a right to a coat-of-arms. It's a common misconception that every family has a coat-of-arms or family crest, but the actual coat-of-arms is the personal property of the holder.

The right to bear arms is heritable, so the sons and in some circumstances, daughters of the person who has had arms granted to them, can also use a coat-of-arms. However, only one person owns a particular coat-of-arms, so during his lifetime, sons use a slightly different version of the arms. Such differenced arms have extra charges added to the shield, the colours are changed, or some other modification is made. Only rarely is the crest part of the coat of arms modified, so all the sons have different coats of arms that include the same crest. In England at least, no crest has ever been granted that was not part of a coat of arms.

This day and age, instead of carrying around shields emblasoned with a coat of arms, you will every so often see a gentlemen with a signet ring on their little finger, the coat-of-arms or cress engraved in. I usually spot this while people-watching on my daily commute.

The College of Arms is the official heraldic authority for England, Wales, Northern Ireland and much of the Commonwealth including Australia and New Zealand. They are responsible for the granting of new coats of arms, the College maintains registers of arms, pedigrees, genealogies, Royal Licences, changes of name, and flags.

I contacted the College of Arms in London, and shared some emails with a William George Hunt, an officer of arms. I sent William a family tree tracing back to my ancestor Thomas Knowles of Gillingham, who was born in 1577 and who is well documented in William and Jill's work. Unfortunately, according to their records, we do not have a direct right to arms, at least not back to 1577 anyway, however, William's research did bring up some other points of interest, the two emails are as follows;

29th January, 2014

Dear Mr Knowles,

Thank you for your letter and cheque of 8 January.

I have now made a search in our records for all the pedigrees and grants of Arms to persons named Knowles and its variant spellings.

There is only one record which might relate to your pedigree (Norfolk 5.148). This is a pedigree of Cox and includes a marriage on 30 May 1721 between William Knowles and Mary Cox, daughter of Joseph Cox. The entry for William Knowles reads as follows: "William Knowles of Ryarsh in the County of Kent one of the two sons of Thomas Knowles of the same place mentioned in the Will of Henry Cox in 1732. Died 4 October 1766 aet: 77". She died 3 April 1734 and was buried at Ryarsh, where there is an MI.

They had five children, two sons and three daughters. The eldest son, William Knowles of Roughway Wrotham, co. Kent, (PCC will dated 5 January 1802) married Elizabeth Newman and they had offspring. The second son, Henry, died a bachelor and intestate on 31 May 1813. There is no mention of a son John. The three daughters were Mary, Barbara and Eleanor. The Cox family was armigerous but the Knowles family was not.

If you are interested in petitioning for a grant of Arms, please let me have a copy of your or your father's CV so that I may determine whether you are eligible. The fee for a grant of Arms and Crest is £5,250.

Yours sincerely,

William Hunt
Windsor Herald

30th January, 2014

Dear Mr Knowles,

Thank you for your e-mail of yesterday.

I have now investigated the Cox Arms as illustrated on the pedigree to which I referred (Norfolk 5.148) and have to report that Mary Cox would not have had a right to them as they were not granted until 27 February 1822 (Grants 33.142). They are blazoned Barry of ten Or and Azure three Escutcheons two and one Gules each charged with a Horse salient Argent. Crest: Upon a Helm with a Wreath Or and Azure A demi Horse Argent charged on the shoulder with a Thunderbolt proper. I cannot photocopy or scan this and so you will need to make an appointment to see it if you wish – but you probably do not wish to now.

MI means "memorial inscription" – either a plaque in the church or a gravestone.

Parish registers are accurate in my experience. The mistake you have made is believing someone else's research without seeing the evidences! Never believe what someone else has transcribed – one of my great-

grandfathers who was a vicar is recorded in the on-line version of the 1881 census as "Ken" whereas his name was Jabez (the person who transcribed this misread Rev as Ken). The other thing to remember is that infant mortality was great (I have another great grandfather who was the third son named George by his parents, the first two having died). I see you have lots of Johns and Williams, and they in turn may have named their children John and William. There were probably half a dozen of each born around the same time in the same area; proving which was which can be difficult, especially if there are no wills. I therefore suggest that you see what proofs your relative found. The pedigree was probably compiled before the present wealth of material was available on the internet – but the internet is only a guide to assist you to know where to go to see with your own eyes.

When we record a pedigree, supporting evidences have to be supplied, and the pedigree is examined by two Officers independent of the one acting for the client. They have to be satisfied that the pedigree could be proved beyond reasonable doubt. Your Mary Knowles née Cox may have had a son John who was not included on the pedigree here, either because the genealogist did not come across him or the person recording the pedigree decided to exclude him for some reason.

I see that your pedigree records a couple of descents from Cox, which is quite a coincidence when the pedigree on record here includes a Knowles-Cox marriage. It is therefore worth investigating further. Given that the Cox family on record here married into other families with Arms, they may have been more well-to-do than the Knowles family, and so it is worth investigating whether they left wills.

Yours sincerely,

William Hunt
Windsor Herald

William raises some questions regarding the direct descendants on the family tree, in particular the association with the Cox family. While there is every possibility he may have stumbled across a genuine inconsistency, the tree has been thoroughly researched by three independent sources, Harry Thomas Rogers, William Albert Knowles and Jill Florence Maura Clowes, all of whom have visited churches, parishes and joined family history societies - and their research is all consistent.

William does perhaps raise a valid point, not to necessarily believe the research of others and to *"see the evidence for your own eyes"*, but this book is really just a guide, some first-person accounts to maybe inspire future generations of the Knowles family to continue our research so they can add, update or revise it.

Ancestry DNA testing

Ancestry.com. In November 2016 I took the Ancestry.com DNA testing kit at a special offer price of £49.99. The team at Ancestry claim to have visited many different countries around the globe and collected DNA from indigenous people to form their database.

The Ancestry test involved me supplying a small tube of saliva and posting it to a laboratory in Dublin, Ireland. About four weeks later I recieved my resuts; **Ireland 46%, Western Europe 45%, Great Britain 9%.**

The **Ireland 46%** result was not a huge surprise. My maternal grandparents, Bartholomew Patrick Roche b1908 and Kathleen Cremin b1920, immigrated from Cork to Gravesend, Kent in the 1940s because my grandfather was offered a job there. I'm told they also seriously considered immigrating to America.

My mother's ancestry goes back many generations in Cork, Ireland. The Roche family and the Cremin family can both be traced to the early 19th century. On June 30, 1922, during the Irish Civil War, the Public Records Office of Ireland, located at the historic Four Courts in Dublin, was severely damaged by fire resulting in the loss of a huge number of records; very frustrating for Irish geneologists. Regarldess of this, I think I can assume that my heritage in Ireland goes a long way back. The name Roche in particular is of Norman origin. The Normans arrived in Wexford (145 miles from Cork) in 1169 to help the Irish king of Leinster, Diarmuid MacMurrough. They were invited by Diarmuid to help him fight his enemies and regain his kingdom in Leinster.

The **45% Western European** and **9% Great Britain** results most likely accounts for my fathers side, The Knowles family, including all of the other family names that run into it. That's where things get interesting, because we can trace a definite line back almost 500 years in Kent, England, and the maternal lines running into the family do not account for any Western Europeans that I can see, so perhaps much earlier ancestors migrated to Britain at some stage? The first wave of immigration started after the ice age, 9000BC. They arrived by land bridge from Germany and Belgium, and by boat from France.

What is also interesting is that purely based on my DNA results the website Ancestry.com has matched me with other distant Knowles relatives, from second to eigth cousins! One includes a Robert Voll who noticed we had a DNA match and messaged me. It turns out that we share the common ancestor John Knowles b1777 (my fourth great grandfather and his third). The site also matched me with Dallas Wolf, with whom I share the common ancestor Edward Knowles b1836. Dallas also took the same test, his results came out as **41% Great Britain, 22% Scandinavia, 15% Europe, 11% Iberian Peninsula.** My second cousin Ivan, with whom we share the same great grandfather, Edward Knowles b1860, also took the test, his results were **87% European, 5% Scandanavian, 8% other regions.** We were accurately matched as second cousins.

23andMe. In April 2017 I took 23&Me DNA kit test priced at £149.99. Like Ancestry, 23&Me had formed their database by visiting areas around the globe and collecting samples. The test required a sample of saliva sent to a lab in the USA

My results were as follows **80.1% British & Irish, 6% Scandinavian, 12.2% Broadly Northwestern European, 1.2% Broadly Southern European, 0.3% Broadly European, 0.2% Southeast Asian.** Much to my surprise, 2.8% of my DNA is from Neanderthals! The average 23andMe user has 2.7% DNA...

My results have matched me with 1,010 DNA relatives (Other 23&Me customers) of British and Irish origin, 890 of French and German, 705 of Scandinavian before diving straight down to 195 Eastern European, 165 Iberian, 115 Italian, 80 Balkan. These results strongly support the Ancestry test.

My paternal haplogroup is identified as R-M222, which is a subgroup of R-M269. A paternal haplogroup is a family of Y chromosomes defined by a particular set of genetic variants. My haplogroup tells me about my paternal-line ancestors, from my father's to his father and beyond. R-M269 is said to be 22,000 years old and its region is Europe. My maternal haplogroup is U5b1c.

So, as for the Knowles family, it certainly looks like we are predominantly a family of European origin.

Knollys Rose Ceremony

Much has been written about Sir Robert Knollys in this book and the likelihood that we are in some way descended if not direct descendants. Jill and I have both conducted separate research with the help of William's original work and we are both confident there is a very strong connection.

To briefly recap, Knollys was an important English Knight who led many campaigns into northern France, serving the King of England, Edward III. While Robert was a hero at home, he was a villain abroad. Often accompanied by possible blood relative Sir Hugh Calveley, he lived by means of plunder, pillage, taking hostages, demanding ransom, protectionism and causing death. He was also notable for his activities in Northern France in the 100 years war, his contribution to the building of a bridge over the River Medway, the setting up, with others, of the Bridge Trust and Charitable donations towards hospitals. Robert is described as small in stature, but a tough and skilled warrior and, though of few words, a skilful diplomat. Robert was born in North Mimms, Hertfordshire in 1312 and died August 1407 in Sconethorpe Manor, Norfolk.

Sir Robert Knollys was, to say the least, a very ruthless soldier in the wars in northern France in the 14th Century. He came home an even wealthier man than when he left England.

To put some of his ill gotten gains to good use, he and Sir John de Cobham paid for a new stone bridge across the river Medway at Rochester when the original Roman bridge was destroyed by ice and flood. The bridge was built between 1387-1391.

In addition, with the King's permission, they set up a Rochester Bridge Trust to ensure the maintenance of the bridge was secured for years to come. Apparently some of their wealthy friends, including one Dick Whittington, gave land as well as money so that rents from properties provided extra income.

The bridge lasted until 1856 when it was replaced by the present Victorian road bridge. The Trust still very much exists and in addition to its original purpose, it is a leading source of engineering education nationally.

Something else Robert is perhaps most well-known for is an annual event that takes place every year in June known as the The Knollys Rose Ceremony. The ceremony commemorates an ancient City judgement dating from 1381. Sir Robert Knollys owned a house on Seething Lane. He was sent abroad to fight alongside John of Gaunt. While he was away, his wife is reputed to have become annoyed with the chaff dust blowing from threshing ground opposite their house, so she bought the property and turned it into a rose garden.

She also built a footbridge over the lane to avoid the mud, but without the equivalent of planning permission. The penalty was that a red rose 'rent' from the garden had to be paid annually to the Lord Mayor. The rose payment was no more than a peppercorn rent, a symbolic fine upon Sir Robert, a leading citizen and a successful and respected soldier.

For this payment permission was given *"to make an haut pas of the height of 14 feet"* across the lane. The footbridge has long since disappeared, but the legal requirement for the payment of this quit-rent has been established as one of the City's traditions.

On Wednesday, 14 June 2017, I attended the Robert Knollys Rose Ceremony and luncheon with Jill.

Jill and I began our day at All Hallows Garden by the Tower, where a red rose was picked by The Master of the Watermen and Lightermen, Mr John Salter and placed on a pillow. From there we walked along with other guests in an orderly line to Mansion House, where we enjoyed a drink while the rose was presented to the Lord Mayor of London, Mr Andrew Parmley.

After the reception at Mansion House, we set off to the Company of Watermen and Lightermen at St-Mary-at-Hill in the City to enjoy a three course meal with the other guests. It was at this point that we were introduced to more guests, they were genuinely very excited to have Knowles present at the event. Apparently the last time a Knowles/Knollys attended was four years prior.

Jill and I gifted the Watermen and Lightermen a first edition copy of the Knowles Family book, which they were delighted to receive. In a speech after the main course, the head of the Watermen pointed out that Knowles were present and thanked us for the book. One of the highlights of the meal was a speech by a Russell Cooper, Warden at the Rochester Bridge Trust that Sir Robert co-founded.

"The first bridge across the River Medway at Rochester was built by the Romans soon after the invasion in AD43. It lasted for many centuries until, in 1381, the River Medway froze solid. When the thaw came, the ice and floodwater swept away the old Roman Bridge. Luckily for Rochester, two benefactors soon arrived on the scene and arranged for the building of a new stone bridge and chapel. Perhaps even more importantly they persuaded their friends and acquaintances to donate land and money for the perpetual maintenance of the bridge. In 1399, King Richard II allowed the appointment of two Wardens

to care for the bridge and its assets and the Rochester Bridge Trust was founded.

Six hundred and fifteen years later, the Trust is still going strong….still providing bridges at Rochester free of charge to the public, using the proceeds derived from the assets given by our donors at the end of the fourteenth century. I am the latest to hold the position of Senior Warden in an unbroken line of wardens from 1399.

So, who were those donors that built Rochester Bridge and, through their foresight, ensured that we can still carry on the work 6 centuries later? One of them was the very same Sir Robert Knolles that we are here to commemorate today.

Sir Robert was an important English knight who made his fortune in the Hundred Years' War. Born in Cheshire in about 1325, Knolles first appears as the captain of several castles in Brittany in the mid-14th century. He was a convenient ally to Edward III and the Black Prince as he was happy to do their "dirty work" in France in return for the fortunes he could pillage and blackmail – and was enormously successful in it. For example, without Knolles' successful diversionary campaign, it is hightly unlikely that the Black Prince could have succeeded in his legendary Poitiers campaign. In return for his support, the English Crown was content to let him wreak havoc throughout the north of France and build up his fortune as he went. His methods, however, earned him infamy as a freebooter and a ravager: the ruined gables of burned buildings came to be known as "Knolly's mitres".

Robert Knolles was ruthless with his own men as well as the French. On more than one occasion, feeling himself under threat from the French armies he marched away with his own retinue, leaving the bulk of the army to be comprehensively defeated and slaughtered.

Sir Robert was back in England in time to take a characteristically robust part in suppressing the peasants' revolt. This timely service in June 1381 earned Knolles the freedom of the city, a title he proudly boasted in his will.

War had made Knolles a wealthy man and he was also a generous man. He was prepared to share the spoils of war freely with his own men and his friends. But Knolles also proved astute and converted some of his resources into property as well as doing a healthy business in loans to the Crown and associates in the city.

After 1381, with advancing years, Knolles's attentions turned more obviously to charitable and religious foundations. He received a licence in 1389 to visit 'the Roman court for the quieting of his conscience' and founded a hospital and almshouses at Pontefract. A contemporary considered that he decided to make the enormous financial contribution to building the 500 feet long stone bridge across the River Medway at Rochester "meaning in some way to make himself as well beloved of his countrymen at home as he had been every way dreaded and feared of strangers abroad"

Rochester Bridge Trust Warden, Russell Cooper

Jill and I were both pleased to have attended the Sir Robert Knollys Rose ceremony. It is a well organised event and traditions like these really give London its sense of character and wonder. Above all, our possible links as a family to Sir Robert made this even more special.

We hope that one day, stronger links will be found.

Sir Robert Knolles (circa 1325 – August 15, 1407)

A painting of the Combat of the Thirty (March 26, 1351), Sir Hugh Calveley crawls from the battlefield. Sir Robert Knolles lies unconscious in the background

Sir Hugh Calveley (died April 23, 1394)

A french print. Another view of the Combat of the Thirty. Sir Robert Knolles is battered down

Effigy of Sir Hugh Calveley (died 1394), St Boniface's Church, Bunbury, Cheshire

The Knollys Rose Ceremony

The picking of the rose at All Hallows by the Tower

The rose is cut

On route to Mansion House

The event draws many spectators

The rose is delivered to the Lord Mayor of London at Mansion House

The Lord Mayor of London, Mr Andrew Parmley with the Watermen and Lightermen

Edward and Jill with Mr John Salter, the Master, of the Watermen and Lightermen

The Freemen's Room at Watermen's Hall

Possible line of ancestry before 1577 based on William's research

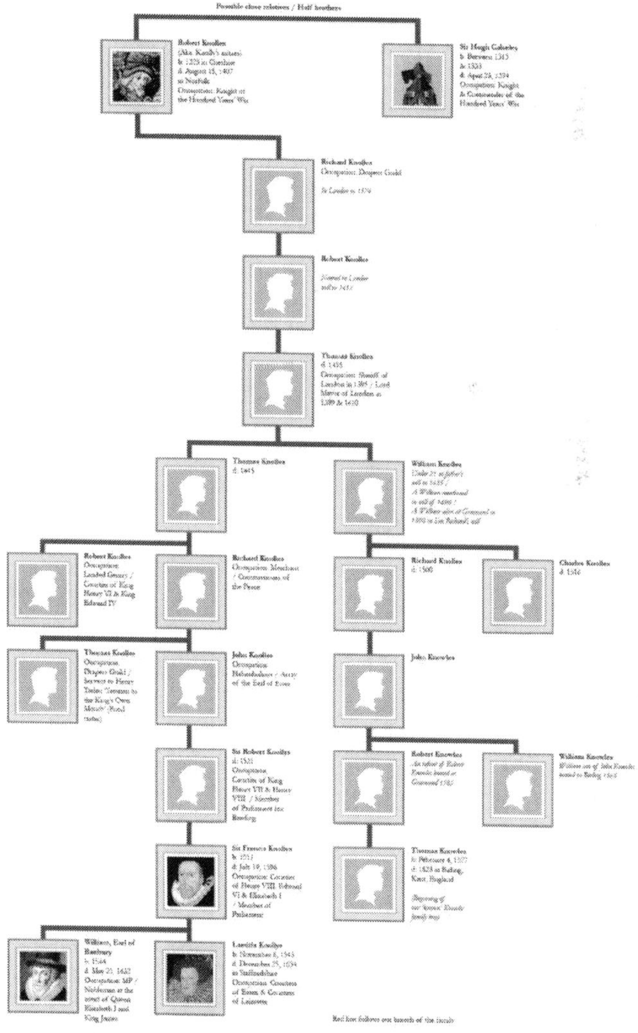

Possible line of ancestry before 1577 based on Jill and Edward's research

We have started from an ancestor of whom we have confirmed records – Thomas Knowles born 1577.

The following information has been taken from Ancestry.com trees and various other sites that either give details of individuals or family lines. However, accurate data and citations on websites and trees seem few and far between unless the individual was particularly noteworthy for some reason.

It should pointed out that even historians cannot always agree on certain issues. For example, one will write *"left no heirs"* where another might record sons predeceasing their father. In the latter instance, it would seem evident that a grandson was an executor of the will.

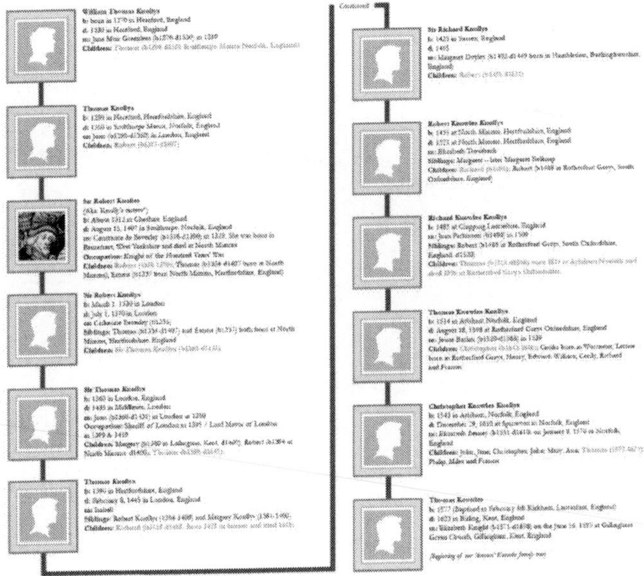

The original of this photo had "Edward Knowles 1802' written on the back by an unknown. If that were true, it would make this photo of Edward and presumably his wife Mary Wildish (b1806-d1871) the earliest known Knowles photograph (regarding our line of Knowles). Fashion experts from Kings College London, the Costume Society and the Victoria and Albert Museum have verified this photo as taken sometime in the mid to late 1870s. We believe that this is more likely to be Edward's son, Edward, who was born in 1836 and his wife Mary Anne Wiles born 1838

Edward Knowles (b1836)

Horace Knowles

Douglas Knowles

MR. KNOWLES CALLS IT A DAY

In 1864 Mr. Douglas Knowles' grandfather took charge of Milton Post Office. In 1918 his father became postmaster there and in 1932 it was the turn of Douglas himself to carry on the family tradition at the High Street sub office.

But on Friday the tradition ended - and this week there were new faces behind the counter of the post office which had been in the Knowles family for 106 years.

For on Friday Mr. Knowles retired after 38 years as postmaster. Aged 69, he had worked in the post office from the age of 15.

ENJOYED

"And I've enjoyed every minute of it", he said "I've nothing at all to regret".

Mr. Knowles a man who knows Milton like the back of his hand - "I should write a book called 'Seventy years in the High Street'," he joked - has no intentions of severing all connections with the district even though he has made his home in West Ridge, Sittingbourne.

"Of all the stunts in Milton over the years I don't think there was one I wasn't connected with", he said.

During his retirement he will act as chairman of Sittingbourne and Milton Primary Schools Committee.

Dozens of cards wishing him well in his retirement arrived at the Knowles' home last week, including one from the chairman of Sittingbourne Council, Cllr. James Buckey.

And one customer paid this tribute to the former postmaster:"Mr. Knowles was more than a postmaster, he was a friend and helper to everyone. We feel that we are losing someone very precious in Milton history".

Mr. Knowles — he'll have more time for gardening now. NE.3380

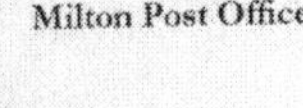

Milton Post Office

Ramsgate

Margate

Faversham

Ramsgate

Canterbury

Faversham, 79 Preston Sreet on Coronation Day, 1911

Uplees fruit pickers

39 High Street, Whitstable

Herne Bay

Whitstable

Faversham - 79 Preston Street

1946 1966

KNOWLES

PRICES

assure that all housewives will have a

Very Happy Christmas

and the most pleasant and

Prosperous New Year

KNOWLES OF MARGATE

(Proprietors M. and H. TUTT)

KNOWLES FOR FRUIT

NEXT TOWN HALL.

Buy Our Kentish Cherries

These Cherries I offer you are Kentish grown Cherries from our own orchards, and are freshly picked and sent me three times daily direct from the orchards.

Buy Our Kentish Cherries, and be proud of them.

DON'T BUY FRENCH !

KENTISH GROWN WHITEHEART CHERRIES—4d. and 5d. lb.

KENTISH GROWN BLACKHEART CHERRIES—6d. and 7d. lb.

1,000 FRESH CUT CUCUMBERS—4d. and 5d. each.

PLUM TOMATOES—3d. lb., 2 lbs 5½d.

FINEST TOMATOES—9d. lb.

LOCAL GROWN GARDEN PEAS—8d. gallon.

BUY KENTISH CHERRIES !

KNOWLES FOR FRUIT

Edward Knowles, Jun.,

(LATE KNOWLES & SON,)

WHOLESALE AND RETAIL

English & Foreign Fruiterer,

And GREENGROCER,

PRESTON STREET.

ALL KINDS OF FRUIT OBTAINED TO ORDER

The Talk of the Town.

Giant Cooking Apples,

8d. gall.

2d. lb.

KNOWLES & SON,

COVENT GARDEN, Whitstable.

KNOWLES *for*

Fruit Salads Vegetables Cut Flowers

FRESH DAILY

Edward Knowles Ltd.

79 PRESTON STREET

Tel. Faversham 2107

Wholesale and Retail Fruit Merchants and Growers

Distributors of Produce throughout the Kingdom

Have

Healthy

Looks

EAT MORE FRUIT

Knowles for Fruit

Telegraphic Address—}
Knowles, Faversham.

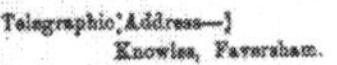

Telephone—8y Faversham.
85y Dover.

FRUIT.

In present circumstances we feel in no mood to be frivolous. War has been forced on us owing to Germany ignoring the treaties of Europe. We are glad to inform you that the English fruit crop is one of the best on record; in fact we don't think ever we have had such record crops all in one year. Our Uplees Fruit Farm is a full crop of Apples, Pears and Plums, and it is our intention to sell them from our shops at Faversham, Whitstable and Dover at low prices.

Fruit the Best Food.

Fruit the Cheapest Food.

To-day's Prices.

FRUIT for Cooking:—

Morella Cherries, 1½d and 2d per lb.
Lovely Apples, 4d. and 6d. gallon.
Plums, 6d. and 8d. gallon.
Stewing Pears, 8d. gallon.
Tomatoes, 2d and 3d lb.
Lemons, 1d. each.

Fruit for Dessert:—

Hothouse Grapes 1s 3d and 1s 6d lb.
Yellow Melons, from 6d each.
William Pears, 1s. and 1s. 6d. doz.
Ripe Bananas, 7 for 6d.
Ripe Plums, 2d. per pint.
Small Pears, 1d and 1½d. pint.

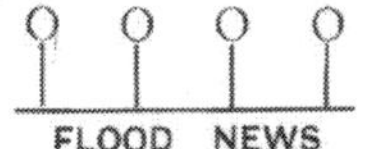

FLOOD NEWS

PRESTON ST. AFFECTED

BELISHA BEACONS AFLOAT

RESIDENTS HAPPY AND BRIGHT

"OUR" CORRESPONDENT VISITS THE AREA

Thursday

Floods seem to be the order of the day and Faversham was not to be left untouched.

Strangely enough, Preston Street (owing to its high level) is the centre of the flood havoc and the whole town must within a few days become affected.

"Our" correspondent paid a visit to the area to-day, and was amazed at hundreds of Belisha Beacons floating by and the cheerful spirit of everyone in the vicinity.

Shoppers were carrying on as usual, in fact the majority seemed more heavily laden than ever.

Our correspondent was anxious to know "Why the heavier shopping"? "Were the shoppers anxious to get home before their own houses were flooded"? But he found that most of the shoppers were anxious to flood there own homes! This seemed a paradox, until, after further inquiries, it transpired that the Preston Street flood was a trifle different to those raging in other areas. The fact was that Knowles, of Fruit Fame, had a flood of Fruit for Sale and what had been thought to be Belisha Beacons were actually some **Fine Jaffa Oranges** and Knowles tells us he is selling them **1½d. ea., 10 for 1/-**. Really we have never seen quite such value in our lives. This is where fruit will save your [illegible] as well as your health. Hold one of these high in the air and any oncoming vehicle will stop immediately!

Jaffas were not alone, there were Grapes 5d. lb., 2 lbs. 9d.; Red Rosy Apples, beautiful flavour, 3½d. lb., 2 lbs. 6d.; Denia Oranges 16 and 20 for 1/-; Fine large Egyptian Dates 3d. per lb.; Grape Fruit 2d. each; Spanish Onions, 3 lbs. 4d.; as well as a fine arrival of Marmalade Oranges 14 for 1/-.

No wonder the shoppers were heavily laden, they enjoyed bailing out the flood, and flooding their homes!

Shop at Knowles; you don't need boats—just big baskets, or let Knowles send it.

KNOWLES FOR FRUIT

KNOWLES for FRUIT

1536	1936
[illegible]	[illegible]

KNOWLES for FRUIT

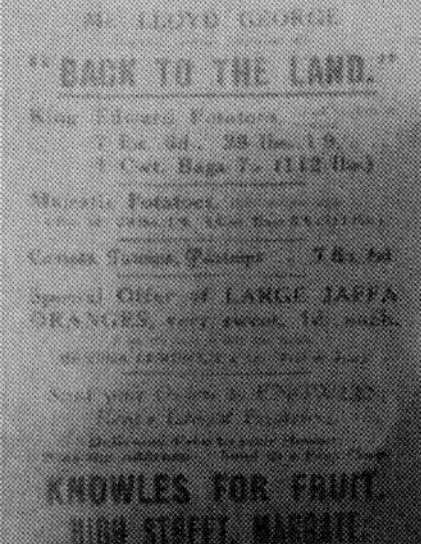

Potatoes! Potatoes! Potatoes!

You Must Bring Your Own Bags.

1½D lb.

AT

Knowles & Sons,

COVENT GARDEN, Whitstable.

KNOWLES FOR FRUIT
NEXT TOWN HALL.

40,000 Slaves to the Council.

KNOWLES FOR FRUIT

THE BEST NEWS FOR YEARS.

Potatoes 5 pounds for 6d., 10s. cwt. Grand Cookers.

Spanish Onions 2½d. pound, 5lbs. a Shilling.

Large Denia Oranges, 1d. each, 7 for 6d. Extra Large Oranges 1½d. each, 9 for 1s.

Only 2 more Tons of Dates left. 4½d. pound, 3lbs. Shilling. Buy them quick.

Lemons 1d, and 1½d. each. 5,000 Boxes Tunis Dates, 10d. Box.

Tomatoes 1s. 3d. pound. Bananas 2½d. each, 5 a Shilling.

KNOWLES,

FAVERSHAM, WHITSTABLE, DOVER,
ABERDEEN, DUBLIN.

Looted! The fate of a florist's establishment in Grafton Street.

Grafton St Shop probably in the 1910s

'Your Old Friend, Knowles'
Edward Knowles (b1860)

Harry Knowles, Mayor of Faversham - official photo, circa 1950

Douglas Knowles, Chairman of Sittingbourne Council 1952/53 & 1953/54 - official photo

Barry Matthew Knowles
1964 -

Written in 2017

The following is a brief summary of the history of the Irish branch of the Knowles family based on my personal knowledge, family stories and some more recent internet research.

James Pankhurst Knowles (1868 – 1944)

Early Life in Kent

My great grandfather James Pankhurst Knowles was born in Milton Regis, Kent in late 1867 or early 1868, the seventh of 13 children of Edward Knowles and Mary Ann Wiles. He was named after his maternal grandmother Frances Pankhurst and her father James Pankhurst.

As a child he lived in the family home at 56-60 High Street, Milton Regis, where he is recorded as a three year old in the 1871 census and again in 1881 as a 13 year old scholar.

New Business in Aberdeen

It is said that James originally intended to work in the civil service. Instead he and his brother Charles moved to Aberdeen at a young age to establish their own business. The Knowles Food Services website, current owners of the business, says it was founded in 1886 by Charles Knowles.

The earliest reference to the business that I have been able to find is a newspaper ad from July 1887 which lists Knowles & Son Kentish Fruit Growers operating from the New Market. A start date in 1887 with both Charles and James involved from the beginning is supported by comments made by Charles at a function in 1937 to mark the 50th anniversary of the business.

The Aberdeen Post Office Directories list addresses of various properties used during the following two decades. The earliest entries are in 1888, listing the Knowles & Son *"fruit growers"* business with three city centre addresses. The locations changed a number of times in the early years.

Marriage and Family

James married Charlotte (Lottie) Longley in Milton-next-Sittingbourne, Kent between July and September 1889. They had six children, all born during their time in Aberdeen: James Charles Edward (Jim) was born in 1890, followed by Charlotte Mary (Lottie) born 1892, Sydney (my grandfather) in 1896, Sarah Ellen (Nellie) in 1898, Arthur Balfour born in 1905 and Percy Durland in 1907. James was a member of a Masonic Lodge.

Aberdeen Expands

Knowles & Son opened a retail shop in Union Street, the main shopping street in Aberdeen, in 1889. James is listed in the Aberdeen directories for the first time in 1891, described as a *"fruit auctioneer"* as distinct from the fruit growing operation, and with a separate business address. From 1892 onwards both brothers are linked to the Knowles and Son business.

The Union Street shop must have been successful because in 1892 a second shop was added at the far end of the street. The business is now described as *"fruit growers and importers"*. A *"wholesale office and warehouse"* was added in 1894 and after a few moves this settled in Exchange Street from 1897 onwards.

From 1896 the business name was changed to Knowles and Sons (plural), perhaps acknowledging a change in the partnership, or maybe just for marketing spin! A telephone line, Aberdeen 548, was installed in the office in 1898 and more lines were added in the other locations over the following few years. Nurseries at Airyhall a few miles to the west of the city are first mentioned in 1905.

By 1895 James and his family were living at 34 Gladstone Place which is the ground floor apartment in a two-apartment building. The 1901 census records the family at this address together with their housekeeper Mary Reilly aged 16. Later that year they moved to the more spacious upstairs apartment, 36 Gladstone Place, where they remained until 1908.

Move to Dublin

In 1908 James moved with his family to Dublin to establish his own fruit and florist business. The family were all living at Rochester, 23 Terenure Park, Terenure, Dublin at the time of the 1911 census, together with Kate Lee, a 16 year old *"general domestic"*. This remained the family home into the 1920s.

A shop at 27 Grafton Street was opened on 9 July 1908. Grafton Street was, and still is, the premier shopping street in Dublin and this was to remain the main location for the business throughout its life.

In February 1909 a branch was opened at 6 Lower Sackville Street (now O'Connell Street). It would seem that the branch was not successful as it is no longer mentioned in ads after November 1910. This was probably fortunate as the location was devastated during the 1916 rebellion.

Decade of Change

A turbulent decade of Irish history began in August 1913 with the Dublin Lock-Out, a major industrial dispute lasting five months which involved 20,000 workers and 300 employers. The family business traded through this period and a newspaper article in November reported:

"Mr. Knowles, of Grafton street, seen yesterday, said that personally, though he was not affected by the holding up of traffic at the North Wall [Dublin Port], saw that it was a very serious matter for Dublin, particularly those engaged in the fruit trade, and who had not the facilities or had not made arrangements, as fortunately he had for getting in large stock. He was one of the few that got in six weeks' supply order to meet a situation such as this afternoon developed. He had enough stuff in hands at the present moment to take him well over Christmas, no matter how large the demands."

In December 1914 Knowles & Sons acquired the business of a Mrs Ryan who traded as McCluskey Fruiterer & Florist in nearby William St. The additional business was transferred to the Grafton St shop where they *"acquired additional premises immediately adjoining their own … [to] almost double their present accommodation"*. This most likely refers to acquisition of the adjoining premises at 1 & 2 Lemon Street, around the corner from 27 Grafton St., and which was used for the wholesale business.

1916

In January 1916 they acquired the business and shop premises of James Delaney, 24 Upper Baggot St. A mews in nearby Clyde Lane was used as a van garage.

During the Easter Rising in April 1916 the area around St Stephen's Green at one end of Grafton Street was taken by rebels, whilst Trinity College at the other end of the street was the main staging ground for the army. As a result Grafton St was in a no-man's land and a number of the shops including Knowles were looted by people living in tenements in the neighbouring back streets.

The looting is mentioned in news articles and also in documents which were recently collected and published in official events marking the centenary of the Rising.

• *"A Citizen's Diary" column in Irish Times 2 May 1916: "Thursday [27 April]. To town at 2.30 p.m. Military shooting from TCD up Grafton street, evidently to stop looting in that quarter. The gutted condition of Knowles's shop (fruit and vegetables) explains the crowds of women and girls from Longford street and Mercer street and adjacent lanes, carrying home orange boxes with fruit, potatoes, bananas, apples, etc., etc. Boys in the raided (Knowles's) shop "lifting" all they can, in spite of the bullets going past, and even occasional rushes across the street with the plunder. At the back of Knowles's vegetable shop are stores, and here an army of slum girls and women were hurrying away with bundles of stuff, while scores of women were meeting them on their way to the source of supply. No interference with this industry. Home by Mercer street, an orange and banana saturnalia – Knowles's – hundreds of people on the streets, animated and jolly."*

• *"Irish Life"* Record of the Rebellion. (p11): *"On Thursday morning [27 April] the top of Grafton-street was the scene of operations. During the night of Wednesday the corner sweet-shop was raided, but on Thursday morning, shortly after eight o'clock, as I was passing through, the work was being started methodically and in real earnest. I found afterwards, however, that the looters were unable to get further down the street than Knowles' fruit-shop. The street here makes a bend which brings it within view of the roof of Trinity College, and I was told that a rifle volley definitely put an end to the industry as far as Grafton-street was concerned."*

• Nenagh News, 6 May 1916: *"In Grafton street also the looters were busy until a few shots from the military sent them all scurrying to their lairs. Amongst the Grafton street houses which have suffered by the marauders are … Knowles fruit store".*

• Diary of Dorothy Stopford Price, 1 May 1916: *"Grafton St looks much the same except for Knowles which is a wreck, and all the windows have bullets through them".*

• Letter from Wesley Hanna to his family, 2 July 1916: *"In Grafton St the mob looted Knowles (fruit shop) Leverette and Fry's, Woolworths, Kapp and Petersons, Noblettes and Maison Phillips."*

Whilst all the stock was taken and the fixtures & fittings largely destroyed, the looters were unable to break into the office safe containing *"cash, books and valuable documents"* which were recovered intact.

While the shop was being repaired, customers were advised to deal with the new Baggot Street shop. Grafton St reopened on 6 May with limited stock.

The Property Losses (Ireland) Committee was established to compensate for losses due to the uprising. James filed a claim of £1879 for stock and fittings lost during the looting and was eventually awarded £1385. The reasons for the deductions were never fully explained to him despite correspondence throughout the following year. Details on the official file, which was made public a century later, show £279 of the deductions to have been completely arbitrary.

The business does not seem to have been significantly affected by the Great War except that some stock which would normally be imported was sourced locally instead. On a personal level there must have been concerns for my grandfather Sydney who was posted abroad with the Royal Engineers.

1920s

The business appears to have recovered and thrived despite the civil and political upheavals that took place into the early 1920s. By 1926, barely 3 years after the end of the troubles, the family business was advertising in *"An t-Oglac"*, the official newspaper of the new Irish Army, pitching to supply food to the barracks … *"Write for our special weekly list for army messes!"* As well as running the family business James was a successful stock market investor throughout this period.

1930s

In November 1930 the adjoining premises at 26 Grafton Street were acquired and merged with the existing shop. The new space was used to expand the floral side of the business and all works were completed just in time for Christmas. By 1931 the family were living at Milton Regis, 33 Orwell Park, Rathgar in Dublin and this remained their home until Charlotte's death in 1959.

The following year, 1932, saw the start of six years of turmoil for fruit importers caused by a trade war between Ireland and Britain, which resulted in very high duties being charged on imports. James was an outspoken critic on the issue and was quoted several times in the papers.

The Dublin and Aberdeen businesses were run as a Scottish partnership between Charles and James until 1936. I am not aware of any day-to-day interaction by the brothers in each other's locations after the move to Dublin, though newspaper ads routinely included the tag line *"also Kent London and Aberdeen"*. The partnership was dissolved on 2 September 1936 with Charles taking sole control of the Aberdeen business and James taking the Dublin business.

Charles would have turned 65 years old during that year and James was 68 so this may have been connected with their planned retirement. JP did not completely retire at that time however, and remained active as managing director of the business until his death.

References in the weekly newspaper ads to the Baggot Street shop also cease from September 1936 with all business being done through 26/27 Grafton Street from then on.

The only family photo that I have of JP and Charlotte dates from around the time of their golden wedding anniversary in 1939. Three generations are present: James and Charlotte; daughters Lottie and Nellie; Arthur with his wife Gertie and daughter Shirley; Percy with his wife Kitty and son Nigel; Sydney's wife Mildred and their son Dudley (my father). My grandfather Sydney presumably took the picture. JP's eldest son Jim and family are absent as they were living in England by this time. The photo is included in a later section of this book.

Latter Years

Although Ireland was neutral in the 1939-45 war, imports for the shop were severely restricted. In the early 1940s Knowles apologised to customers that *"supplies [of oranges] are short and dear temporarily"*, with a promise that larger and cheaper supplies would arrive shortly. In 1941 the firm switched to selling Irish-grown produce instead of imports where possible.

James was in his usual good health when he left Dublin in late June 1944 for a holiday at the Grand Hotel in the nearby seaside town of Greystones Co. Wicklow. Three days later, on 1 July 1944, he died there of a heart attack aged 76. He is buried in Kilternan cemetery only a couple of miles from my current home, along with family members from the following two generations.

James left an estate of £77,000, the equivalent of more than £3million in current day terms. In his will he set up a trust the main purpose of which was to provide for his widow and unmarried daughters Lottie and Nellie for their lifetimes.

Charlotte Longley (1865 – 1959)

Early Life in Kent

My great grandmother Charlotte (Lottie) Longley was born in Rainham, Kent on 31 December 1865 and she was christened there on 25 February 1866. She was the third of eleven children of Charles James Hoy Longley and Sarah Ellen Gearren. She was named after her paternal grandmother Charlotte Hollands.

In the 1871 census Charlotte, aged 5 years, is recorded in the home of Walter Gearren, a 63-year-old farm bailiff, in Luddenham, Kent. On the original census form Charlotte is described as Walter's niece. Walter's wife Mary and sister-in-law Ann, both also in their sixties were also there, as were a domestic servant and eight unrelated boarders who were farmworkers mostly aged in their late teens and twenties. In fact Walter and Ann Gearren were not her uncle and aunt – they were her maternal grandparents. Charlotte's parents and all their other four children were at their own family home in Rainham at the time. I wonder why Charlotte was not with the rest of her family – did she just happen to be visiting that night, or was she living with her grandparents for some reason?

In the 1881 census Charlotte, now aged 15, is recorded at 9 Preston Street, Faversham, Kent, and is described as a

Confectioner's Assistant. The head of this household was George Smith, aged 57, a master baker employing one man and one boy. George Smith was Charlotte's uncle, married to her father's sister May Longley. Also recorded at the same address are George's two staff (including his nephew), and two other nieces who were draper's assistants. The Smiths do not appear to have had any children of their own. It seems likely that Charlotte was living there whilst working for a confectioner in the town.

Marriage and Move to Aberdeen

The year 1889 brought major changes in Charlotte's life. The Longleys had been fruit growers and "nurserymen" in Rainham since at least 1825 and elsewhere in Kent since at least 1780 and would have known the Knowles through trade over a prolonged period. Charlotte married James Pankhurst Knowles in Milton between July and September 1889. Charlotte's mother died within a few weeks of their marriage.

By this time James had established the Knowles & Son fruit business in Aberdeen with his brother Charles so Charlotte moved to Aberdeen with him following the marriage. She is recorded at the family home in Aberdeen in the 1891 and 1901 censuses.

Their life together in Aberdeen is fully described in the section about JP Knowles. Their six children were born in there between 1890 and 1907.

Dublin and Later Years

The family moved to Dublin in 1908 and their life there is also described in the section on JP Knowles. She is recorded at the family home in Terenure Park, Dublin in the 1911 census.

Following her husband's unexpected death in July 1944, Charlotte continued to live in the family home at Milton Regis, 33 Orwell Park, Rathgar in Dublin. Her daughters Charlotte (Lottie) and Sarah Ellen (Nellie) lived with her and looked after her faithfully throughout her remaining life. They were all comfortably provided for by the trust set up in JP's will.

Charlotte had broken her hip when she was in her 70s. While on a holiday in England about ten years later she broke the other hip. Following treatment she agreed to travel back to Dublin by air, which was quite an achievement for someone of her age at that time. Although her mobility was impaired she remained mentally very alert well into old age. She died peacefully at home aged 93 on 11 December 1959 and was buried with her husband in Kilternan.

Sydney Knowles (1896 – 1981)

Early Life in Aberdeen

My grandfather Sydney Knowles was born on 10 April 1896 in Aberdeen, the third of six children of James Pankhurst and Charlotte Longley. He was named after another Sydney Knowles, his father's younger brother, who was born in 1873 and died very shortly afterwards.

In the 1901 census Sydney is recorded living in the family home at 34 Gladstone Place, Aberdeen. Later that year the family moved to the slightly larger upstairs apartment in the same building, 36 Gladstone Place.

Move to Dublin

When the family moved to Dublin in 1908 to establish the Irish fruit business they lived at Rochester, 23 Terenure

Park, Terenure. Sydney is recorded here in the 1911 census as a 14 year old scholar (he was just a week short of his 15th birthday).

Great War

During the Great War, Sydney served in the Royal Engineers. I have few details of his service and it appears likely that his service record was among those lost during bombing in the Second World War. I believe he served in Mesopotamia (Iraq) and India. He was a motorcycle dispatch rider charged with delivering messages between officers at various posts. He rode an "Indian" bike and prided himself on his riding skills; I remember him saying that the correct way to get the bike going was to run alongside it and jump on when the engine fired rather than using the kick start. As a child I recall seeing an old photo (sadly now lost) of my grandfather with his Indian; apparently he brought the bike into a photographer's studio to get the picture! Thankfully he was not injured during the war though he did contract malaria which occasionally recurred later in life. He finished the war as a corporal.

In 1922 a War Memorial Hall was built by Rathfarnham Parish. Sydney's name is included in a plaque on the wall commemorating all the men of Rathfarnham Parish who served in the war. There is also a Roll of Honour in Rathfarnham Parish Church which includes his name.

1920s - Marriage and Family

After the war Sydney returned to work in the family fruit and floral business with his father J.P. and his younger brothers Arthur and Percy. On 23 January 1923 Sydney married Mildred Miriam Strouts in Bromley, Kent; they were cousins, their mothers being sisters.

At first Sydney and Mildred lived at 18 Eaton Square, Terenure, which is just around the corner from the Knowles family home in Terenure Park. They remained here until 1927 when they moved to a newly built bungalow at 43 Bushy Park Road, Terenure. They named this house "Milverton", a name they retained for their subsequent homes.

Their only child, my father Dudley, was born in 1929.

1930s

In 1930 Knowles & Sons doubled the size of their Grafton Street shop by acquiring the adjoining premises. The additional space was used primarily to expand the floral side of the business which was run "as a separate branch under a specially trained staff". By 1937 Sydney was in charge of the floral department.

Family holidays in the 1930s were normally taken in the south of England, visiting relatives and at the seaside.

1940s

Following the sudden death of their father J.P. Knowles in July 1944, the Grafton Street business continued as a partnership run by Sydney and his brothers Arthur and Percy. As the eldest brother Sydney was often referred to as the senior partner or managing director.

In 1945 the firm was among the first six florists in the country to join the Florists Telegraph Delivery Association (FTDA), which later became Interflora.

In 1948 the family moved to a new house which had been designed and built for them. Milverton, 194 Orwell Road, Rathgar is in the same neighbourhood as their previous homes. I have some memories of this house from my early childhood. It is in a lovely location overlooking a golf course, with a large back garden and plenty of space.

By 1949 Sydney was on the executive council of the Confectioners' and Fruiterers' Association, when it was reported that trading in the sector had recovered to pre-war levels. He was subsequently appointed treasurer and remained on the council until just before his retirement in 1961.

1950s

By the 1950s Knowles of Grafton Street was a well-known institution in Dublin and appears to have provided a very comfortable living for the three brothers and their families.

During the war years the family had spent their holidays in Ireland, instead of travelling to England as they had done previously. In the 1950s they took a number of foreign holidays including trips to France, Switzerland and Mallorca.

My father Dudley got married in 1958 and Sydney became a grandfather at the end of the decade when my sister Karen was born. Sydney's mother Charlotte died the very next day marking the end of an era for the family.

1960s – Retirement (twice)

In 1961 Sydney turned 65 and, although his brothers were younger, they decided to retire from the Grafton Street business. The shop closed at the end of August and the premises and contents were sold.

A year or so later the family set up a new business, Knowles Import Export Trading, with an office at 63 Upper Rathmines Road in Dublin.

Newspaper ads for home saunas were placed regularly starting in 1963, and later for other items such as massage equipment, intercoms and adding machines. I recall being in the office as a small child when my Dad worked there. The Knowles name was painted in gold lettering on the upstairs window. The business was an agency so it did not require large premises or warehousing as the products were handled by distributors.

By 1967 my grandparents had turned 70 and decided to move to a more manageable house. The third "Milverton" was at 48 Rathdown Avenue in Terenure.

The Rathmines business closed around 1970 when Sydney retired for the second and final time.

Latter Years

I have plenty of personal memories of my grandparents in the 1970s as we visited them every Sunday evening for dinner. Sydney kept up a dapper appearance, frequently wearing a bow tie, and he was very fond of smoking his pipe.

The "bran tub" was a tradition that they kept for us as children each New Year: They would bring a half-barrel, which was filled with sawdust, into their kitchen and then my sister and I would roll up our sleeves to rummage for small gifts and novelties which were hidden in it. I do not know anyone else who did this and often wonder where the idea came from.

In 1973 my grandparents marked their golden wedding anniversary by having friends and relatives (including us grandchildren) to a reception in their house.

In the summer of 1977, and by now over 80, Sydney and Mildred sold their house and moved to an apartment at 2 Vergemount Court, Clonskeagh, Dublin. They were in the apartment only a few weeks when my grandmother became seriously ill and was hospitalised. As they were not able to return to the apartment it was sold again early in early 1978. They moved to Oak House Nursing Home on Orwell Road, Rathgar, which was on the same road where they had lived previously.

My grandmother died that summer and my grandfather spent his final years in the nursing home. He continued to drive for a further year or so and would call over to visit us at the weekends; later my father would drive him over. He died at Oak House on 14 August 1981 and was buried in Kilternan.

Mildred Miriam Strouts (1896 – 1978)

Early Life in Kent

My grandmother Mildred Miriam Strouts was born on 28 September 1896 in St Mary Cray, near Bromley, Kent. She had one brother, Charles Frank (Charlie) Strouts who was two years older. Their parents were Frank Strouts and Sarah Mary Longley.

The Strouts family trace their roots in Kent back to 1619 when their ancestor Reverend John Strowte moved there from Devonshire. Mildred's great grandfather Robert Strouts settled in Milton by 1836 where he was a butcher, and Mildred's father was the 3rd generation in the family business. He moved from Milton to St Mary Cray when he got married in 1893.

My grandmother had an aunt also named Mildred Strouts who was only around 20 years older than her. They may possibly have both been named after a common ancestor whom I have not been able to identify, or maybe the name was just popular at the time. Her middle name was given for her paternal grandmother Miriam Gouge.

The 1901 census shows Mildred, aged 4, as a "visitor" in the home of the Mudd family at 26 Harmer Street, Milton-next-Gravesend. I have not been able to identify any clear connection between these families. The other members of Mildred's family were at their home in High Street, St Mary Cray at that time.

In the 1911 census all four family members were at their home in High Street, St Mary Cray and Mildred was described as a 14 year old scholar. She attended Morville House School at this time: I have a copy of Lamb's Tales From Shakespeare which was presented to her "for reading", at Christmas 1910, signed by her teacher Anna Bowers. The following Christmas she was presented with a copy of the Complete Works of Shakespeare "for general improvement". Miss Bowers was clearly a big fan of the Bard!

Ireland

Mildred would have known the Knowles through her mother's family and connections in Milton-next-Sittingbourne. Her aunt, Charlotte Longley, who was her mother's younger sister, was married to JP Knowles.

On 23 January 1923 Mildred married JP's second son, Sydney, in Bromley. Their life together in Dublin is fully described in the section about Sydney Knowles.

Mildred had only one child, my father Dudley, who was born in 1929. They had a comfortable family life with a live-in household help. My grandparents played tennis in their younger and middle years. They also sometimes played croquet in the back garden and I have recently had their croquet set, dating from around 1930, restored.

My grandmother had her own car, an early 1950s Morris Minor that she was still driving 20 years later.

The house must have become a lot quieter after my father got married in 1958. Their constant companion afterwards was their terrier Shandy. My grandparents had a good social life well into their later years. They played bridge with their friends and neighbours and had an annual get together at their home around the New Year. We visited them for dinner every Sunday throughout my childhood.

Mildred was in good health until the last year of her life. She died aged 81 on 25 June 1978 at Oak House Nursing Home in the same area where they had spent most of their lives. She was buried in Kilternan.

Dudley Frank Knowles (1929 – 1996)

Early Life

My father Dudley Frank Knowles was born in a Dublin nursing home on 28 June 1929, the only child of Sydney Knowles and Mildred Strouts. His middle name was given for his maternal grandfather Frank Strouts.

He grew up at the family home, 43 Bushy Park Road, Terenure, in Dublin.

My Dad attended St Andrews College junior (primary) school which at the time, the late 1930s, was in Wellington Place, Clyde Road, Ballsbridge in Dublin. In the pre-War years family holidays were spent visiting relatives in Kent and relaxing on the beach in Eastbourne.

1940s

Dudley attended secondary school in Sandford Park, Ranelagh in Dublin during the war years, and made lifelong friends there. At this time the family holidayed in Ireland, staying at Kelly's Hotel in Rosslare Co. Wexford where my Dad won a prize for cricket. After leaving school he studied commerce in Trinity College Dublin (TCD) in 1946/47. Following university he joined his father and uncles working in the family shop in Grafton Street. In 1948 the family moved to their new home at 194 Orwell Road. My Dad had a motorbike at this time, so following his father who had been a motorcycle dispatch rider during the Great War.

1950s

My father's parents gave him a new MG TD sports car for his 21st birthday in 1950. This was his pride and joy and it features in a large number of photos which he took over the next few years.

He first met my mother Ursula McDermott in the early 1950s when she joined Knowles & Sons to work as PA to my grandfather. Dudley and Ursula became engaged in May 1958 and were married on 13 November that year.

My parents had arranged to buy a newly built bungalow, which they named Cranford, in Glenbower Park, Churchtown, in south county Dublin. My Dad's parents gave them the house as a wedding present so they could start married life without a mortgage.

Just before the end of the decade their first child, my sister Karen, was born on 10 December 1959.

1960s

Following the closure of the fruit and flower business in Grafton Street in 1961, my father worked in the new Knowles Import business which sold health & fitness equipment and some office machinery. He was still working there when I was born on 15 June 1964.

When the Knowles Import business closed in 1970 my dad had to find a new role. He became a self-employed commissioned agent for Delicon Imports, a company based in west Dublin which imported and distributed confectionery and biscuits from continental Europe. He worked with Delicon until his retirement.

1970s

My parents sold the bungalow in Glenbower Park in 1973 and at the end of July we moved to Arlington, 15 Ailesbury Lawn, Dundrum, just a mile away.

My Dad's main interests were gardening and following the Ireland rugby matches on TV. He also followed motor racing, and he and I would attend the annual two-day motor races in Dublin's Phoenix Park. Throughout the 1970s we spent our annual family summer holidays in the seaside village of Camp in County Kerry – despite its name it was very rural and not a holiday camp!

Being an only child, the responsibility of looking after his aging parents increased in the later 1970s. When my grandparents moved home twice within 12 months in 1977 my parents looked after all aspects of the moves, and my father had the added stress of coping with his mother's terminal illness at the same time. After his mother died in 1978, Dudley continued to be very attentive to his father Sydney. He visited my grandfather at his nursing home regularly after work during the week, and brought him to visit us at home at the weekends.

1980s

The early 1980s were a time of change for our family. My grandfather died in 1981 and my sister Karen got married in 1984. Dudley became a grandfather the following year with the birth of Karen's first daughter, Alison Allen. A second granddaughter, Jennifer Allen, was born in 1987. My parents started taking regular foreign holidays in the 1980s, usually touring in their own car in France.

Final Years

The number of grandchildren increased to four with the birth of Karen's sons Damien Allen in 1990 and Conor Allen in 1994. I married Gerardine Gaffney in 1991.

In April 1993 the business of Delicon was acquired by a company called Johnson Brothers. Dudley continued to work on behalf of the former Delicon business until his retirement just before his 65th birthday in 1994. In his brief retirement he had the opportunity to spend more time with his grandchildren and enjoyed pottering about in the garden.

My father died aged 67 on 1 December 1996. His ashes were interred initially at Rathfarnham Parish Church before being moved in 2015 to rest with my mother's in the family plot at Kilternan.

Ursula Bridget McDermott (1932 – 2014)

Early Life

My mother Ursula Bridget McDermott was born in south Dublin on 13 January 1932 , the youngest of five sisters. Her parents were Matthew McDermott, who was a professional golfer, and Agnes Sara Hughes. My mother's middle name may have been given for her great grandmother Bridget Mary Dalton.

The family home was at 5 Sarsfield Terrace, Main Street, Lucan, Co. Dublin. It is now converted into a commercial premises for a photographer.

Difficult Times

Tragedy struck in 1940 when my grandfather died at home unexpectedly, leaving a young widow and family. My mother was only 8 years old at the time. Very shortly afterwards Ursula was diagnosed with scarlet fever. Today this disease is treated with antibiotics but back then it was considered very dangerous and easily transmitted. My Mum was hospitalised in an isolation ward and many of her favourite toys were destroyed in case they carried the infection. This must have been very traumatic for the young girl and she often talked about it in later life.

Following my grandfather's death I believe the family lived in Bray, County Wicklow for a period though I have no details about this.

Growing up in Dublin

By the mid-1940s my aunts were in their late teens and early twenties and had started their respective careers so there was ample income coming into the household. Ursula was then a teenager and they were living at 67 Lower Leeson Street, Dublin, which is only a few hundred yards from St Stephen's Green park in the city centre. At that time Leeson Street was a residential area in Dublin's famous Georgian quarter. In more recent decades the street became a centre for nightlife and today the house is a well-known nightclub.

1950s – Decade of Change

By the mid-1950s the family were living at Holyrood Castle, Sandymount in Dublin. Ursula was now in her early 20s and she took a job as personal assistant to my grandfather Sydney Knowles at the family shop in Grafton Street. The situation must have become quite awkward when she and my Dad started dating shortly afterwards!

Ursula changed jobs to work as a PA for a well-known dress designer Sybil Connolly whose career was at that time breaking new ground in the US where she was to become designer to celebrities of the day. My Mum really enjoyed this work and I feel that in later life she regretted not taking her career further. She sometimes talked about missed opportunities to join a large accounting firm or to become an Aer Lingus air hostess (this was at the time when air travel was still seen as glamorous!).

Marriage and Family

My parents became engaged in May 1958 and were married on 13 November that year. Their life together is described in the section on my father Dudley Knowles.

My Mum gave up work when she got married. It must have been a big change to spend most of her time at home. My parents' first house, Cranford, Glenbower Park, Churchtown, was in a small road and the neighbours, of all ages, were very sociable and frequently had coffee mornings in each other's houses.

My Mum got her first dog, a West Highland called Heather, in 1959. We had two more Westies in later years and Ursula was to become very attached to her dogs.

Karen was born in December 1959 and I arrived in June 1964. Looking after us and the house filled her time for many years from then on. Spare time was often spent tidying the garden. Every Sunday afternoon we would join her mother, sisters and their families at Holyrood Castle where some of them still lived until the 1980s.

My sister Karen moved out when she married in 1984. Ursula became a grandmother for the first time in 1985 with the birth of my sister Karen's daughter Alison, and three more grandchildren followed – Jennifer, Damien and Conor. After I married in 1991 my parents were alone at home for nearly the first time in their married life.

Latter Years

My father's illness and his death in late 1996 were very difficult for my mother. A few weeks later, just after her 65th birthday, she fell downstairs and suffered head injuries which resulted in her spending the next 2 years in hospital and a nursing home. During this time the house in Dundrum was sold as it would not be suitable for her in the future.

Against all the medical prognoses she eventually recovered sufficiently to leave the nursing home and buy another house - Lislea, Flemingstown Park, Churchtown. This house is very near Glenbower Park where my parents had first lived. By now Ursula had 6 grandchildren following the birth of our children Laura in 1998 and Frank in 2002.

Ursula continued to have difficulties in managing to live alone and in 2004 she moved to Cairnhill Nursing Home, Foxrock where she was relaxed and well cared for. Following a major stroke in 2010 she required constant care but happily was able to remain in Cairnhill. She died aged 82 on 3 November 2014 and her ashes were interred in the family plot in Kilternan.

James Charles Edward Knowles (1890 – 1955)

Early Life in Aberdeen

James (Jim) Charles Edward Knowles was born on 10 June 1890 in Aberdeen, the eldest of the six children of James Pankhurst Knowles and Charlotte Longley. He is recorded living with his parents in Aberdeen in the 1891 census, at that time their only child. In the 1901 census was living in the family home at 34 Gladstone Place, Aberdeen by which time he is the eldest of four children.

Move to Dublin

Jim moved with the family to Dublin in 1908 and worked in the family fruit business. The first Irish Food and Cookery Exhibition was held in Dublin in November 1909 and he was quoted as proposing a vote of thanks by the standholders to the organisers of the show.

In the 1911 Irish census he is now aged 20 and living at the family home, Rochester, 23 Terenure Park, Terenure, Dublin.

Marriage

On 28 July 1912 Jim was baptised at St Joseph's Catholic church in Terenure. He would undoubtedly have been baptised in Scotland as a baby so this second baptism presumably marked his conversion to Catholicism which must have been a controversial step with his family at the time.

Two weeks later on 9 August 1912 Jim married Esther Mary Josephine O'Reilly at the same church in Terenure. Esther was the daughter of James and Honora O'Reilly and her family address is given as 32 Oakland Terrace, Terenure. Apparently Esther was also known as Polly and she was born in 1885.

Jim and Esther were living in their own home at 20 Ashdale Road, Terenure by 1913. They had six children born between 1913 and the early 1920s: James CW, Albert, Brendan, John, Paul and Sheila. Their lives and families are outlined later in this section.

Times of Change

Jim left the family fruit business to set up the first of a number of new businesses that he would own at various times in his life. In early 1922 he opened the Shamrock Toffee Works in Shankill, a south Dublin suburb. He lived nearby at St. Brendan's, Shankill. The company's products were advertised throughout the year as part of a "buy Irish" newspaper campaign and the business employed around 20 people.

Unfortunately political events were to lead to violence later that year when a Civil War broke out between supporters of the newly formed Irish Free State, and Republican "Irregulars". On 26 August 1922 armed Irregulars seized stock, petrol and goods from the factory. They returned on 18 September and took oil, petrol and car parts, and again on 30 September when they removed more stock.

Finally, in the early hours of 8 November the buildings and contents were burned down, and petrol cans were found outside the following morning. Jim was asleep at the time of the fire and woke the next morning to find the factory "a mass of smouldering ruins". In 1924 he was awarded £2040 in compensation for the loss of his buildings, van and stock.

This must have been an immensely troubling time for Jim and his family. Sometime afterwards the family moved from Ireland to England. I do not know the exact date – probably between 1923 and 1935 – nor to what degree the fire was a factor in the decision to move.

A New Life in England

I have little personal knowledge of this phase of Jim's life and perhaps we may learn more from his direct descendants in the future. He maintained contact with his family in Dublin, particularly his mother.

By 1939 Esther, Albert and Brendan were living in the Brentford / Chiswick area whilst Jim was now living with Irene Knowles (born 1891) in Fulham. It would seem that his first marriage had ended and he had since remarried. A marriage between James C Knowles and Irene Lawley in Islington, registered between October and December 1935, may be theirs. More speculatively, a death record for Irene M Knowles, registered in Kensington between July and September 1947, may possibly relate as the year of birth matches as does the location. Irene would have been aged 56 that year. There is also a death record for Esther M Knowles in Ealing between October and December 1950.

During his life in England, Jim set up a number of different businesses. One of these was manufacturing dog coats, which were sold through Harrods. At another stage he ran a taxi business.

By 1955 Jim was living at 3 Talgarth Road, Fulham / West Kensington. The houses at 1-7 Talgarth Road are now combined into a hotel. Jim died at home on 15 December 1955, aged 65.

James & Esther's Children

According to William Knowles' research in the family book, James and Esther had six children:

James Charles William Knowles (1913 – 1983)

James Charles William Knowles was the first child of James CE and Esther. He was born at the family home 20 Ashdale Road, Terenure, Dublin on 7 June 1913. He was named after his father and grandfather, confirming a tradition in this line of naming the eldest son James. He was baptised in the Catholic parish church in Terenure when only 4 days old.

James moved to England with the family when they relocated in the 1920s or '30s. He married Sarah A Magan between July and September 1939 in Hammersmith when he was aged 26 and she was one year younger. James and Sarah managed Kenton House Hotel, Hillcrest Road, Ealing for many years. Their home in 1953 was nearby at 5 Hillcroft Crescent, Ealing.

They had four children:

James W R Knowles (born 1942)

James W R Knowles was born in Hammersmith between July and September 1942 . He is the fourth James in this line of the family. He is married to Phyllis and they live in Ealing where they managed Kenton House Hotel following James CW's retirement. They have three daughters –

Gwendolyn lives in Greenwich; Kerri and Jennifer both live in the USA.

Michael A Knowles (1943 - ?)

Michael Knowles was born in Hammersmith between October and December 1943. He passed away a few years ago.

Maureen T Knowles

Patricia Knowles (born 1946)

Patricia Knowles was born in Hammersmith between April and June 1946. She lives in Ealing.

James CW Knowles died on 26 July 1983 in Ealing.

Albert V Knowles (born 1916)

Albert V Knowles was the second child of James CE and Esther. He was born in south Dublin between October and December 1916. He was baptised in the Catholic church at Haddington Road in Dublin in 1916.

Albert would have been a teenager, at most, when the family moved to England. Following his parents' separation, Albert lived with his mother Esther in the Brentford / Chiswick area in the late 1930s.

Between January and March 1943, now aged 26, he married Mabel V Tyson in Brentford. Mabel was born between July and September 1915 in Poplar, London so she was a year older than Albert. Mabel's mother's maiden name was Miller.

Albert and Mabel appear to have had two children:

Peter G Knowles (born 1944)

Peter was born between April and June 1944 in Brentford.

David R Knowles (born 1947)

David was born between January and March 1947 in north eastern Surrey.

I do not have any reliable information about Albert and Mabel or their family in their later lives.

Brendan Godfrey A Knowles (1918 - 1969)

Brendan Godfrey Knowles was Jim and Esther's third child. His name was sometimes spelt Brendon. He was born in south Dublin on 11 June 1918. Like his brother Albert, he was young when the family moved to England. In 1939, when he was 21, he was living with his mother and Albert in their home in the Brentford area.

Brendan married Teresa Darbyshire in Fylde, Lancashire between October and December 1944. Teresa was born between January and March 1924 in Fylde; her mother's maiden name was Appleton.

Brendan and Teresa had four children:

Wendy A Knowles (born 1946)

Wendy was born between April and June 1946 in Heywood, Lancashire.

Judith M Knowles (born 1947)

Judith was born between January and March 1947 in north east Surrey. She married Peter A Exley in Hounslow between July and September 1968. Peter was born between January and March 1944 in Uxbridge; his mother's maiden name was Seidal. Judith and Peter had three children:

Nathaniel Brendan Exley (1971 – 1999)

Nathaniel was born in Hammersmith on 21 February 1971. Unfortunately he died aged only 28 in Kingston Upon Thames in the summer of 1999.

Benjamin Oliver Exley (born 1972)

Benjamin was born between July and September 1972 in Kingston Upon Thames.

Elizabeth Mary Exley (born 1973)

Elizabeth was born between October and December 1973 in Kingston Upon Thames.

Judith was living in New Malden, Surrey in more recent years.

Brendan Knowles (born 1949)

Brendan was born between April and June 1949 in south Middlesex.

Gregory Knowles (born 1949)

Gregory was born between April and June 1949 in south Middlesex. Brendan and Gregory appear to be twins.

In his latter years Brendan Godfrey Knowles lived at 269 Popes Lane. He died in Hounslow on 20 October 1969.

John Knowles

Paul Knowles

Sheila Knowles (born 1922?)

John, Paul and Sheila Knowles are the last three children of Jim and Esther according to the notes provided by William Knowles as mentioned elsewhere in the book. It has not been possible to independently verify the names.

Two of Jim's sons became Catholic priests and his daughter became a nun – my father's cousin Joy Kayser recalls meeting them in the late 1960s or '70s. These must have been John, Paul and Sheila as we already know the history of Jim's other children. John and Paul were twins. We have virtually no other information about these three relatives.

There is a birth record for Sheila Mary Knowles born in Rathdown between January and March 1922. Rathdown is the administrative area that includes Shankill in south Dublin where Jim and his family were living that year so this is a tentative link but we would need more information to confirm.

Charlotte Mary Knowles (1892 – 1982)and Sarah Ellen Knowles (1898 – 1992)

Early Life in Aberdeen

My great aunts Lottie and Nellie were inseparable throughout their lives.

Charlotte Mary Knowles, known as Lottie, was the second child of James Pankhurst Knowles and Charlotte Longley. She was born in Aberdeen on 27 May 1892. She was named after her mother, and the name Charlotte can be traced back to her great-grandmother Charlotte Hollands. Her middle name may be given for another of her great-grandmothers, Mary Cheeseman.

Sarah Ellen Knowles, known as Nellie, was the fourth child of James and Charlotte. She was born in Aberdeen on 20 February 1898. She was named after her maternal grandmother Sarah Ellen Gearren.

The name Sarah traces back a further two generations to Sarah Tollast. Lottie may well be one of the four young bridesmaids pictured in the wedding photograph of Bernice Harriet Knowles and Andrew Wilson, taken in Sittingbourne in 1899, in the Knowles family book.

In the 1901 census Lottie was 8 years old and Nellie was 3 and they were living at the family home at 34 Gladstone Place. Having spent her childhood in Scotland Lottie retained a distinct Scots accent for the rest of her life.

Dublin

Lottie was 16 and Nellie was 10 when the family moved to Dublin in 1908. By the 1911 census Lottie was aged 18, Nellie was 13, both living at the family home in Terenure Park, and described as scholars.

In 1915 Lottie passed the exams of the Royal Irish Academy of Music to qualify as a piano teacher.

By the 1930s Lottie and Nellie were running a kindergarten school from the family home at Milton Regis 33 Orwell Park.

Nellie learned to drive and she was a safe though cautious driver. At first she avoided taking right hand turns whenever possible, even when this meant taking a much longer route with only left turns! Her brothers took time with her to improve her driving confidence. This must have worked because she was still driving her Morris Minor when she was well into her 70s.

The sisters never married and following their father's death in 1944 they looked after their aging mother at home for the rest of her days. Their mother died at the end of 1959 and the house was sold just over a year later in March 1961. The Trust which their father had set up in his Will provided for their welfare for the rest of their lives.

Later Years

Following the sale of the family home my great aunts continued to live in the same area; firstly at 78A Highfield Road, Rathgar and later in Camross, 35 Dartry Road. I recall visiting them several times at Camross when I was quite young. I also remember visiting them at Christmas in the Standard Hotel in Dublin city centre where they spent the holidays each year. In later years they lived in an apartment at 3 Greenlands, Sunbury Court, Dartry Road.

Lottie and Nellie spent their final years in Glenindare Nursing Home, 202 Merrion Road, Dublin 4. Lottie passed away peacefully in Glenindare on 29 November 1982 aged 90 and was buried in Kilternan with her parents. Nellie stayed on in Glenindare and enjoyed good health for many years. She died in Glenindare on 14 January 1992 aged 93 and was also buried in Kilternan.

Arthur Balfour Knowles (1905 – 1997)

Aberdeen

Arthur Balfour Knowles was born in Aberdeen on 1 April 1905, the fifth child of James Pankhurst Knowles and Charlotte Longley. He spent his early childhood at the family home at 36 Gladstone Place.

Dublin

Arthur was only three years old when the family relocated to Dublin. In the 1911 census he is shown as a 6 year old scholar living in the family home, Rochester, 23 Terenure Park.

In 1921, when he was 16, according to newspaper notices, Arthur was involved in organising rugby matches for Rath RFC. I have not been able to find any other references to this club but perhaps it was connected with his school.

After finishing school Arthur joined his father and his older brother Sydney working in the family fruit and florist business in Grafton Street, probably starting in the mid 1920s.

Arthur had a keen interest in motor sports throughout his life, competing in local events run by the Leinster Motor Club. In 1924, aged 19, he took part in motorcycle trials covering a 64 mile course in the Dublin mountains, though unfortunately I don't know the result! By the late 1940s and 1950s he was a regular competitor in car trials with his MG TD and Triumph TR2 sports cars. In his later years he remained involved on committees of the motor club.

Marriage and Family

On 2 September 1931 Arthur married Gertrude Field (Gertie) in Harold's Cross Church, Dublin. Gertie was born on 4 December 1909 in Dublin. They lived in the south Dublin suburbs, including Dundrum, Shankill and Foxrock.

Arthur and Gertie's daughter Shirley was born in 1936. In 1958 she married Dermot MacDermott. They made their home in Co. Kildare and have seven children: Denys, Shauna, Geraldine, Kieran, Kevin, Bronagh and Stephen. They also have a number of grandchildren.

In 1981 Arthur and Gertie marked their golden wedding anniversary.

Gertie died in her sleep at home on 21 July 1991 aged 81 and left her remains to medical science. Arthur passed away, aged 91, in January 1997 at a nursing home near Shirley and Dermot's home in Co Kildare.

Percy Durland Knowles (1907 – 2001)

Early Years

Percy Durland Knowles was born in Aberdeen on 29 August 1907, the sixth and last child of James Pankhurst Knowles and Charlotte Longley. He was less than a year old when the family moved to Dublin.

In the 1911 census Percy, aged three, was living in the family home in Terenure Park. In the 1920s he joined his father and brothers working in the family shop in Grafton Street.

Marriage and Family

On 3 June 1936 Percy married Florence Lilian (Kitty) Mitchell in Harold's Cross Church, Dublin. Kitty was born in Dublin on 1 August 1914. They lived in the south Dublin suburbs including Rathfarnham, Terenure, Dartry and Foxrock. Percy continued to work as a partner in the family business until it closed in the 1960s.

Percy and Kitty had two children:

Nigel Durland Knowles was born in 1938. Nigel qualified as an engineer and he has lived in Australia since the early 1960s. He married Philippa and they had two children – Geoffrey Durland and Susannah. Geoffrey was my pen pal when we were children in the 1970s.

Cecilie Knowles was born in 1943. She married Ken Read in 1968 and they live in Dublin. They have two children – Tanya and Stuart. Kitty died aged 74 on 7 February 1989 and is buried in Enniskerry, Co Wicklow. Percy passed away on 27 February 2001 and is also buried in Enniskerry. He was 93.

Ivan Keith Knowles
1942 -

Written in 2017

A good deal has been written elsewhere in this book about my great great grandfather Edward Knowles of Milton Regis and my great grandfather Edward Knowles of Faversham, so I shall begin my recollections with my grandfather Charles Knowles – otherwise known as "Clap hands here comes Charlie".

Charles, born in 1893, was the second son of Edward Knowles and Ann Hams of Faversham. He married Harriet Horton and they had three children. The oldest was my father Gordon born in 1914, then followed Eric born 1915 and Hazel born 1920. Charles died in 1966.

Gordon married Phylis Novena Stringer in 1939 and I was born in 1942.

After primary school, at the age of 10, I was packed off to boarding school at St. Edmunds Canterbury until I was 16. I was an acting Lance Corporal in the St. Edmunds School Combined Cadet Force and as a lad belonged to the Sea Scout 2nd. Whitstable Troop.

Leaving school on a Sunday I was put to work in the Whitstable shop on Monday.

In 1960 I joined my father's company Coinmatics – more about that business later – and met my wife Yvonne the same year. Yvonne's maiden name was Edwards her brother being Ron Edwards a well-known business man in Herne Bay. We married in 1964 and have two sons. Our elder son is Paul, born in 1965 and our younger son is Gary born in 1967. Paul and his wife Evelyn, nee Sperring, have two daughters, Lauren Amy born 1988 and Charlotte Lara born 1991

After the selling of Coinmatics I went back into the fruit trade for about a year and then, in 1972, the Whitstable shop became a leisure centre which I ran for 27 years with Yvonne and staff.

In the summer season, I also worked at the arcade on the sea front at Herne Bay which was known as Paul and Gary Amusements. This arcade was eventually sold to Cain Amusements. We also had the Jackpot Arcade on Marine Terrace Margate which is now a Wetherspoons Pub.

Looking back, it was long and unsociable hours, but that was the nature of the business that I was in from 1960 until 2000.

However, we did find time for a social life outside the leisure business for our own leisure. I joined Masonry in 1968, the Rising Star Lodge no. 6153 London, Graystone Lodge Whitstable and Pentalpha Lodge in Canterbury having gone through the chair in 6153 and likewise Pentalpha a few years later.

I was fortunate to be at Wembley to see England win the World Cup in 1966, and Tottenham in the first all London Cup Final against Chelsea.

My father,Gordon, was an astute business man, a careful thinker and planner. He was completely on top of all matters financial, always aware of costs and outgoings and always paid his accounts on time.

A man of good principals, loyal to his friends, his business reputation was to be admired.

He passed on his expertise to me and to my sons with a couple of witty mantras:

"There are only two things you need in life, a good pair of shoes and a good bed, because if you are not in one you are in the other" .

And when making a purchase, property for example – *"Let your eye be the judge, let your pocket be your guide, let your money be the last thing that you part with and line your pockets with pig skin so that every penny comes out with a grunt"* .

My father was a Mason and founder member of Faversham Lodge and their first Chaplain. His Mother Lodge was Rising Star London 6153 which he joined in 1946, attaining London Grand Rank and was in all 33 degrees of the Craft.

In 1996 Gordon was interviewed and the conversation recorded on tape.

The following is an insight to his early life in Whitstable taken from that tape.

He asked his father as a young child where he was born. Charlie's answer was that he was conceived in Faversham Rec after the town carnival, but born in Dover. As the carnival was due to be held the week following the interview the interviewer wished him happy anniversary!

The family moved to Whitstable in 1916 and Gordon attended Westmeads Infant School and clearly remembered the names of his teachers and the Maypole dancing.

His father then sent him to Wrieghts School Faversham which by the time of the interview was the old Queen Elizabeth's school for boys. He was a monitor and recalls the first few names on the register he was charged with calling. He admits to ticking names off whether they answered or not!

He wanted to leave school at 14 and help in his father's business. He goes on to describe the type of produce they sold and the previously mention habit of buying fruit on the tree.

He wanted to earn more money so his father told him that he would have to do more work. He started making up bobbing which was basically bundles of wood. He went around the general stores in the town and sold 100 bundles to a shop on Island wall for six shillings. He soon had such a demand for his bobbing that he could not get enough wood.

His Thursday afternoon job for his father was to break up the blocks of dates into one or two pound bags. His father would come and check the weight just to be sure they were correct.

His father Charlie bought one of the first National Cash Registers and, apparently, that took quite a bit of getting used to. One advantage being that Charlie could hear every time the till was opened!

In the interview he names just about every shop and business on Whitstable High Street, sometimes recalling which ones owners had the prettiest daughters. At that time the

High Street was a grit road and in the summer the council sent horse drawn water tanks to help lay the dust. Eric and Gordon liked following the truck to get their shoes wet. They played marbles in the gutter on their way to school and did not like the stink of paraffin that came from Tommy Coleman's general store.

He sometimes went with his father to a house that contained the telephone exchange. Charlie did not have to give the operator a number, just said "I want to talk to Edward Knowles of Faversham".

Eventually Charlie decided he could afford a telephone and his number was Whitstable 123.

Gordon remembers his father going to Brighton and being very impressed with a new attraction, a mini golf course. He decided this would be a money spinner in Whitstable and bought some ground near Hamilton Road. He had a large wooden shed built and all the equipment for an 18 hole mini golf course installed. There was at the time a famous golfer named A B Mitchell and as it so happened Charlie had a man of the same name working for him. The adverts for the new attraction stated that you could come along and meet A B Mitchell! In spite of all his efforts Whitstable was not ready for Mini Golf – not one of Charlie's better investments.

Gordon said he and his father were close and he certainly taught him how to make a living. Gordon would be up at 4am off to London's Spitafield's market with lorries to take the produce back to Kent. He used to park his car just off Petticoat Lane and got to know a local Jewish tailor. Sometimes as he returned to his car the tailor would call out "I have a suit for you Knowlesy". These suits had been ordered but not collected, usually because the customer had died. Gordon maintained he still had one in his wardrobe bought fifty years ago and never worn.

My father had bought his first automatic coin machine (polite term for a one armed bandit) and dabbled in the early years finding one or two sites where they could be placed such as cafes etc. and using the old penny as the price of pulling the handle. The legality of these machines was doubtful and varied from local authority area to area. Some were lenient, some were not, so one tended to duck and dive a bit in those days.

In 1958 a new betting and gaming act was passed in Parliament and machines first started to appear in pubs, not using cash but brass tokens purchased from behind the bar priced at 6d each, 2.5p in today's money. Tokens won and jackpots were then cashed in for goods only (beer, wines or spirits).

My father traded under the name Coinmatics and in 1960 he formed the company Coinmatic Whitstable Ltd. with Stanley Bradley, Reg Butcher and myself, each of us putting in £250. The business flourished throughout the sixties supporting eleven of us as my father's brother Eric had joined us with his company. We were supplying machines to Whitbread Fremlins, golf clubs and cafes, and in all about 400 pubs throughout Kent and East Sussex with a hand full in London. We sold Coinmatics to a company called Pleasurama, a public company operating casinos in London, Ramsgate and the Isle of Wight. They merged us with a company from Charing called Selecta Music which had already been acquired by Pleasurama.

My father had been the main instigator in all these business transactions as well as still running the fruit shop and farms.

On February 26th 1972 he lowered the shutters on the fruit shop for the last time. He turned to the leisure industry and opened again as a Leisure Drome. *"Clap Hands Happy Days are here again"* read the advert in the Whitstable paper. There are photos elsewhere in this book of Gordon carrying a sack on his shoulders and waving goodbye to his customers.

As well as opening the amusement arcade/ leisure centre in the old fruit shop, another was bought in Herne Bay and another on Margate seafront.

Last word quoted from Gordon's taped interview, *"I should have been a journalist I would have made more money"*

Gordon died in 1999.

Eric the second son of Charles and Harriet Knowles married Sheila Tappenden (1914-2012). They had three children, Michael Charles born 1942, Patrick born 1948 and Charles Edward born 1951. Eric's second wife was Vera Waller nee Draper. Eric died in 2006.

Michael married Mavis Reynolds and they have two daughters, Michelle born 1970 and Emma born 1973. Michael runs a Health Food shop in Whitstable with the help of his second wife Sue Bishop and Michelle.

Patrick married Jean V Ward and they have two sons, Steven born 1979 and Barrie George Edward born 1982. Patrick's second wife is Ann Bailey.

Charles Edward the third son of Eric and Sheila Knowles was born in 1951 and married Janet Butler they have two children, Adam born 1984 and Natasha born 1988.

Hazel was the youngest child of Charles and Harriet Knowles. She married Mervyn Leonard Tutt and they both died in 1979.

The information above brings the descendants of my grandfather Charlie Knowles up to date. Now for my recollections of the man who was larger than life and sometimes just as unpredictable.

Charlie was born into a fruit growing, retailing family and must have been used to helping out in his father's Faversham shop from an early age. However before turning to the family trade he was in the army stationed at Dover during the 1914-1918 war.

He was a keen cricket player and played a lot with officers. On one occasion an officer asked Charlie to take his uniform to the local cleaners to be cleaned and pressed as there was an important parade coming up. On his way to the cleaners Charlie popped into a local professional photographers and had his photo taken wearing the officer's uniform. So not all family portrait photos can necessarily be taken at face value it seems!

Another cricket related story concerns Charlie playing for Lord Harris of Belmont's team. The batsman hit the ball near Charlie and Lord Harris called out *"Your ball Knowles, get it"*, to which Charlie replied *"ok Harris"*. His Lordship retorted *"it's Lord Harris to you"*. Charlie replied *"you are Lord Harris off the pitch not on it"*. I don't believe that he played for his Lordship's team again.

Once Charlie was established in his own shop he attended most hard fruit sales and sometimes managed to cause uproar. On one occasion the auctioneer asked for someone to start the bidding, which Charlie did at 6 pence! After the laughter subsided he made a more realistic bid of £500.

These sort of antics are quite reminiscent of his grandfather Edward's banter with the auctioneers at Covent Garden years before. (Detailed earlier in this book under Peep Shows of the Past).

Knowles's always believed in advertising their products and, as has already been explained elsewhere, Edward of Faversham made an art of the process. Charlie probably obtained the best free advertising available whilst at a cup final at Wembley well before the second world war. He got a mate to phone the football ground from Whitstable with the following message. *"Will Charlie Knowles fruiterer and greengrocer of Whitstable please leave the stadium and return home immediately as an emergency has arisen"* . How to get a free advert listened to by 50,000 people and still stay and enjoy the match!

At one of the local council meetings he attended he became so frustrated that he aired his grievance then stormed out of the council chamber. As it happened the key was in the door, so he locked the councillors in and phoned the London Evening News to tell them what had happened. No one seems quite sure how long it was before the councillors were rescued!

He decided to build some bungalows with timber from the Wembley Exhibition and call them Wembley Villas. He did not apply for planning permission and there was no power or water supply so the council made him pull them down. I believe for a while afterwards his lorries didn't just say *"Clap hands here comes Charlie"* they also displayed *"oh my poor bungalows"*. Charlie never forgave the council for their actions and from that time on he always took every opportunity to publicly criticise them.

As well as the shop in Whitstable High street and the wholesale rounds Charles Knowles Ltd owned a farm at

Fishpool Bottom between Canterbury and Littlebourne, about 70 acres. Also Downs Farm Yalding and Shingle Barn both at the top of Yalding Hill. Charles and Harriet's home was a house appropriately named *"Jaffa"*. It was off the High Street at Whitstable and Muriel Dell mentions in her childhood memories visiting her aunt and uncle there. (Muriel's mother Annie was Charlie's sister).

In the late 1950s Charlie joined Jack Scott and Bill Griggs of Scott and Griggs Ltd. and formed a new company Scott and Knowles Ltd. Once again a little bit of family history repeating itself because Edward of Milton Regis also diversified in later life and bought a builder's company.

So it can be said that Charlie was a mostly successful business man – he won some he lost a few- but mostly came out of his wheeling and dealing a winner.

Also in the 1950s, 57/58 as I remember, Eric and Gordon, Charlie's two sons bought the amusement arcade at 11 Neptune Terrace Sheerness. Eric named it K's Kasino and we used the name again in 1972 when we opened ours – K's Kasino Whitstable.

The casinos catered for all needs. Not only could you gamble, you could eat, drink use the cash machine if necessary and generally have a good time even if you didn't always win!

Around the late 1940s early 50s my father Gordon and Harry Knowles senior were directors of a brush company in Faversham called *"Betta Brushes"*, which I understand went to the wall – Kaput!

This might be a good juncture to mention Harry Knowles's family who I don't believe have been expanded on elsewhere in this book.

Harry was the son of Edward of Faversham and Ann Hams. He was born in 1901 and died in 1975. He married Nellie Harris and they had four children.

Harry Knowles junior 1923-2011 married Lorraine (aka Barbara) Turner in 1948.

He later formed a partnership with Brenda Farmer who had worked in Harry senior's shop. They had three children, Heather, Lesley 1962 and Graham.

Colin Knowles born 1927 married Rosemary Phipps in 1952. They had four children, Isola 1954, Angelina 1957, Joelle 1961 and Tristram Stuart 1968.

Isola married John Partridge in 1984 and they have three children, Zachary Oswald Partridge 1985, Esme Partridge 1986 and Oscar Partridge 1989. According to public record the first two were registered in the Canterbury area and Oscar in Nottingham.

Angelina married Dermot P. Ryan in 1985 and they have three children. Feargal Diarmuid Ryan 1986, Tieman Patrick Ryan 1991 and Ruaidhri Joseph Ryan 1988. The births are registered in Loughborough, Nottinghamshire and Leicestershire.

Joelle married Christopher Cowley in 1983 and they have four children, Mark Anthony Cowley 1981 registered in Northallerton: Christopher John Cowley 1985 registered in Pontefract : Samantha Josephine Cowley 1987 Northallerton and Collette Joanne Cowley 1990 Northallerton.

I have no further information about Tristram.

Harry and Nellie's elder daughter is Mary Knowles 1933 and she married Michael G Woolf in 1957.

They have three children, Julia Woolf 1961 Dylan Woolf 1957 and Kathryn Woolf 1959.

Dylan married Ellen Toenders and they have two children, Mary Rhea 1992 and Carmen Maria 1995 both births registered in the Canterbury area.

Kathryn married Robert May in 1994, I believe they have one son, Felix George May born 1995 in London.

The younger daughter of Harry and Nellie Knowles is Prudence born 1942. Prudence married Peter Latham who is a sculptor and painter. They have two children, Anabell 1962 and Alexis 1965 whose birth was registered in Newport Monmouthshire.

There is a charming photo of Harry and Nellie's 12 grandchildren taken in the gardens of Whitstable Castle on the occasion of their Golden Wedding celebration in 1972.

Moving on from my digression into Harry Knowles family I return to the family of Charlie Knowles.

My uncle Eric has a separate section in this book written by his son Patrick. However, one little story I feel I must include is about his Home Guard Service during WW11. He was stationed at the Battery at Seasalter where ammunition had been going missing for some time. The Sergeant put Eric in charge of the ammunition store with a padlock and key. Eric could not believe his luck – he was the one who had been taking ammunition to go down the marshes and shoot rabbits! Typical dad's army and typical cheeky Knowles!

Charlie and Harriet's only daughter was Hazel. Hazel married Mervyn Tutt. Mervyn was taken prisoner of war in the early years of WWII. During those years Hazel worked at Shorts, Rochester as many women did helping the war effort.

After the war they ran the Margate shop for her father eventually buying the business from Charles Knowles Ltd and then traded in their own right. They sold the premises to Currys and retired to Cliftonville in a bungalow named *"Golden Ours"*. Hazel and Mervyn were a couple who enjoyed life and lived for each other. Mervyn's health gradually deteriorated and rather than be separated again they committed suicide together in 1979.

The Knowles family going back several generations have been involved in Market Gardening, Fruit growing, farming, wholesale and retail trades, post offices and now fruit machines – I think our great great grandfather was absolutely correct *"you have to have push in business and you have to keep moving forward"* (from Peep Shows of the Past – local paper in 1930s.) Makes one wonder what he would have made of all his descendants?

Patrick Knowles
1948 -

Written in 2006

Eric James Knowles 1915-2006. Eric was born in Dover, on 5th November 1915. It was Dover because his father Charlie was drafted into the war, but fortunately stayed this side of the channel as he was required for his Cricketing skills on behalf of his regiment. Whilst he was stationed there Charlie's father got him to manage a fruit shop, as he was only busy weekends, what a beginning to Eric's life.

First World War over, the family returned to Whitstable and Eric began his education and start in life in a very different Whitstable to what we know now. It was traditional in Whitstable at school to be given a nickname and Eric's was Wormus, because he couldn't sit still, a trait that lasted for most of his life. As a young lad he joined the Sea Scouts, Boys Brigade, and the traditional Boy Scouts, it was the Sea Scouts he enjoyed the most, meeting at Goldfinch's Sail loft in Sea Wall to practice on his drum.

At 12 years old Eric regularly drove the family business lorries and his love of any form of motorised transport, particularly motor cycles lasted all of his life; he was driving right up to his recent illness. When he worked at Herne Bay he drove there from Whitstable, always by way of the Herne Bay Bends because it was more interesting than the Thanet Way, no straight roads for Eric.

During the 2nd World War he enlisted to enter the RAF, he couldn't wait to get his hands on a Spitfire and have a go, but as a farmer he had a reserved occupation and was desperately needed at home so that didn't happen. During the war he married his first wife Sheila, and apart from family life, helping to assist in the family business, he was in the Home Guard as a Dispatch Rider on a Motorcycle, what a surprise!

After the 2nd World War was over life returned to some sort of normality but for Eric it was another chance to resume his motorcycling, particularly Grass Track Racing. He was beginning to win now and making a name for himself amongst his great friends like the Arter Brothers from down the road, Grey Brothers, Hallets also Brothers and many more individuals. He raced at Brands Hatch before they made it tarmac, he held the all time Sheppey Grass Track lap record and will for all time as the track doesn't exist any more. When lack of spare time eventually forced him to change from Grass Track Racing to Motor Cycle Trials, his last bike that he rode in competitions was an Ariel 500cc Red Hunter which he kept and used until quite recently.

Moving on to the 1960's Eric's life changed dramatically, his business interests moved away from the Fruit Shops and towards Fruit Machines, same words, totally different.

At the same time his first marriage had failed, but he was to marry his beloved Vera and to move from Whitstable to Sheerness. The Machine Business, particularly the Bingo Side was his niche; to see him sorting and polishing his show prizes was like sorting fruit in the shop display, bruises side down! To see him trying to attract punters to the game, was just an adaptation of selling fruit to customers, politeness, charm and a little persuasion! The Amusement Arcade was named K's Kasino and with Eric at the helm it prospered and went from strength to strength, this was his time for his cars; Triumph TR's, Mercedes Sports, a couple of Rollers, before he settled with Ford Grenada Scorpio's, and of course they being a little sedate, he compensated the Fords with a Harley Davidson Motor-cycle. Later on Eric appeared on BBC TV Regional News item showing viewers his love of his Harley, this being filmed in the Arcade and along Sheerness Promenade. During this time he was made a life President of The Sittingbourne Motor Cycle Club of which he had been a member of since before the 2nd world war.

Another passion for Eric was his annual jaunt to Jersey in the Channel Islands, he originally went there in the early 1950's in a bi-plane with his old friend Fred Hardgreaves, the man who introduced him to the Bingo Business. Jersey had a special place in his heart, and the changes in the Island from all those years ago to the most recent visit in May of this year, must have been tremendous. He also liked to go up to Blackpool, for the lights and to check up on the opposition, see what the latest trends were. Whilst there he would go the Pleasure Beach and have a go on the latest racing coaster i.e. Pepesi Max, last year he was refused a go due to his age, this didn't stop him he went back when they had changed shifts and luckily the next guy wasn't as strict, so he got his ride on the biggest racing coaster in the UK.

On his birthday last year the 5th November, well it would be, he visited The Bonfire Burn up an important last Grass Track Race Meeting of the season, and it absolutely poured down with rain; but with a prior Bells Whisky and Stones Ginger Wine inside, he endured the terrible weather and thoroughly enjoyed the meeting with friends and family around.

These are a few reflections of Eric, and only a fleeting glimpse of him. Eric lived, loved and worked with a passion, that cheeky twinkle in his eye, a boy in his heart all his life, he will be sorely missed.

"Never stop being a kid. Never stop feeling and seeing and being excited with great things like air and engines and sounds of sunlight within you. Wear your little mask if you must to protect you from the world but if you let that kid disappear you are grown up and you are gone." **Richard Bach, 'Nothing By Chance'**

Sydney Clark
'Knowles, Greengrocer, Faversham'
Published in Bygone Kent

Written circa 1985

"Yah! Taint fair.
Thruppence a pound, it said.
Not goin' ter pay."

So showered the critical comments of the indignant queue of thirty or forty customers outside the sixteenth century gabled shop, 79 Preston Street, Faversham, of Knowles, greengrocer, on that Saturday morning at the end of July 1922.

The target of the comments, Edward Knowles, founder of the business back in the second half of the previous century, smiled benevolently - for he was a kind man, as we boys knew - and continued to weigh pounds of cherries on the balanced scales. As another load of cherries arrived from his Uplees Farm, he had just changed the shop notice from *"Fresh Cherries 3d lb. All Ripe"*, to *"31/2d lb."*

"If all you are rushing for a bargain, they must be worth a little more", he told the critics. And business went on as merrily as usual, for he also was gifted with kindly humour. And customers paid up.

They knew they were worth it. For they were Kent cherries. And as I have indicated, the cherries on sale that Saturday morning came from the firm's local farm, at Uplees in the Luddenham district for he was not only a retailer, he was also a grower and wholesaler. "*From our own farms*", was a statement of fact, for not only at the well-known Uplees, but elsewhere, as at Throwley on the other side of the town, did he farm.

And the selection of the Uplees for cherry cultivation reveals the acumen of Mr Knowles, for it marches with Teynham, of which William Lambarde wrote as long ago as 1570, *"the Cherrie garden and Apple orchard of Kent ... Tenham is the parent of all the rest, and from whom they have drawn the good juice of all their pleasent fruite ... where our honest patriote Richard Harrys* (Fruiterer to King Henrie the 8) *planted by his great coste and rare industrie, the sweet Cherry, the temperate Pipyn, and the golden Renate"*. Lambarde says that about 1533, Harrys *'obtained 105 acres of good ground in Tenham'* and planted it with *"plantes from beyonde the Seas"*. A Brass placed in the vestry of Fordwich Church read *"1570. Here lies the mortal remains of Mistress Harris. The wife of the QUEEN'S MAJESTES FRUITERER"*.

The value of the area for cherry cultivation is said to be in the clay and brick-dust soil. It is central to a Kent brick-building district, Sittingbourne to Faversham. Camden (1551-1623) declares *"Kent abounds in cherries beyond measure"* and that they were brought into Britain originally *"about the year of Christ 48"*.

And here is Edward Knowles selling the fruit from the Farm in that same area in the twentieth century, at his Faversham business, which lasted well for 100 years until, after being run by his son, Harry, it ceased trading in September 1965.

Edward was born at Milton, near Sittingbourne, in the 1860s. His parents had a shop there, and Father was one of the first sub-postmasters. In the general shop they also made sweets, baked bread and retailed fruit. Eventually he rode with Father in a pony and van around that part of Kent delivering the mail, but they came to combine that with consignments of fruit.

In a sense, the future of the Knowles greengrocery businesses, which eventually had branches throughout Kent, at centres such as Faversham, Canterbury, Whitstable and Herne Bay, as well as Dublin and Aberdeen, was born on one of these early pony and van journeys. One Thursday they noticed some attractive plums in one of the gardens on their route, and got down and negotiated with the owner to purchase them as a growing crop, with themselves responsible for picking, and selling the fruit. Eventually the deal was struck at £5, but since father and son did not have that money between them, the reckoning was fixed for the following Monday, by which time there had been picking, and selling of plums in the Milton shop, and the debt was discharged.

But this business must have been in their blood, for Edward's youngest brother, who was also born at Milton, went up to Scotland and founded the firm of Knowles and Son, fruit merchants in Aberdeen, with many shops. He died in 1951 at the age of seventy-nine, having left Kent sixty-one years earlier. Edward died in 1929, and his son, Harry, continued, as I have indicated, the Faversham business, while another son, Charlie, ran the Whitstable shop, which had been founded in 1906, and was followed by his son Gordon. In fact, they were so much into fruit, that their Whitstable home in Canterbury Road was named 'Jaffa House', after the orange, of course.

Anyhow, I did not intend to detail the family story here, but rather to highlight an outstanding feature of the family, which was a factor in making them and their businesses well-known over a wide area, and was, I think, outstanding in the era and in advance of their times. That was their advertising and publicity ability, both for their goods and points of view, for they were in local politics as well.

Modern advertising, with all its technological advances, has nothing on the way in which the Knowles expressed themselves with simple, factual straightforward expression in word and print.

For years their weekly advertisement in the Faversham paper was a prominent feature, and was read eagerly by many, including my grandparents, both Clarks and Hadaways, and my parents. With its comment often on matters of interest as well as goods advertised, it was a regular source of interest. I think at times it could have sold the paper.

Here's a simple illustration to begin with. It is dated 4th January 1913, and it is worth noting how it is phrased so that everyone may feel included with their needs met, and there is a suggested remedy for a common 'After-Christmas' feeling. There is even a free gift at the end. We may be intrigued at the prices, but the prophecy of modern method is what captivates me. After the business heading, it goes on:

'FRUIT FOR THE NEW YEAR
We can suit all.
If you want QUALITY, we have it.
If you want QUANITY, we have it.
If you want QUALITY and QUANTITY combined, we have it.
Sweet oranges 16, 24, 30, 40, and 50 a shilling.
Messina lemons16 and 24 a shilling.
Ripe bananas 16 a shilling.
If you are tired of Christmas Pudding and want a change, Buy English Cooking Apples from Uplees Fruit Farm. Wellingtons 6d a

gallon.
Large Greenings 4d a gallon.

Cherry-picking basket - 'Kibsy' or 'Kipsy'.
Secured round waist: flat side on picker's back. Holds 12 lbs.
Small Greenings 3d a gallon.
Remember we want to push on the Apple Trade.
And to every purchaser of a gallon of our apples, we will give a Jumbo Orange."

Simple? Yes. That's part of the art. Effective? No doubt about the meaning. All right, here's a longer example, in which Edward seeks to convince readers of his point of view of the production and sale of food, which will, of course, favour the customers. I said just now that the family was into local politics. Well, they were into national and international politics, too, if the occasion required, and were never afraid of taking on the highest in the land, if they dissented. From the 'Faversham and North East Kent News' 16th August, 1919.

"Telegraph Address Knowles Faversham. Telephone 87 Faversham, Fruit Farms at Uplees near Faversham, and at Nailbourne, Lynsted.
'FRUIT. The Latest Humbug Profiteering Bill 1919.
My dear Reader, Really! Really! Really! Government methods make a man, with his eyes only half open, laugh outright. They always try to Sugar-Coat the Pill for the British Public to Swallow.
'Now the public are crying out about high prices. Government put through the House with all the speed a profiteering Bill and are spending £75,000 on the same in hopes of blinding the Public.
'Who made you pay 2/8d a lb. for your tea? The Government!
'Who made you pay 1/6d a lb for your cheese? the Government!
'Who made you pay 2/6d a lb. for your butter? The Government!"

So this long indictment of the Government goes on - the disgrace of potatoes at 13d a Ib: sugar 6d and 7d a Ib: dates

6d: currants 10d: raisins 11-.
And then, *"Who fixed the present high prices of coal? jams? and made you pay 2/6d a lb. for bacon unfit to eat?
Any of you can see, if you wish to do so, the Government returns about a fortnight ago, shewing many millions of pounds made by the government on articles of food, and large revenue from excess profits. PLAINLY SHOWING THE GREATEST PROFITEERS OF THE AGE ARE THEMSELVES".*

He has stated his case. But he always wanted action. Readers must write to the Ministry of Food, and say *"WE DEMAND SUGAR at manufacturers' prices, so that we can make our own jam"*. Then a word of advice, *"I shouldn't bother to pay the postage ... just put your name and address.!"* The second piece of action required is *"Yes. You're right - buy the good cheap fruit from Knowles, as 'Dessert Plums 6d and 8d per lb: Hothouse grapes 3/- per lb: Choicest Extra Large Yellow Melons 1/9d and 2/- each"*, and so on.

There was lots more: how much it cost that week I cannot guess, but I do know he had a very wide readership. I have mentioned the family's continual involvement in local affairs. Edward's controversy over the cost of water at his premises is an example. He fell out with the local water company, particularly, it seems, because other shops across the road appeared to pay less, such as the Fleur-de-Lis opposite. Failing to secure some adjustment, he refused to pay, and when the matter was reported in the local press, he cut out the reports and posted them in his shop for customers to read. He then cut off his own water supply, and arranged for shop assistants to go each morning and bring back supplies from public pumps. Usually they took buckets, but one report mentions the use of a milk churn on the fruit vehicle.

Both the town pump on the north side of the Guildhall, and another near the Swan Inn, are reported to have been used. It seems that the town pump was not in use, but Edward insisted that the council make it available as citizens had the right to its use. It was a pump which had replaced a leaden pump originally installed in 1635. Had Mr Knowles used it in its early days, he would have been under further expense even for that water, because a Corporation Order about 1645, demanded that *"the neighbours who fetch the water from the pump do keep the same in repair!"*. The iron pump, with an ornamental handle, used by Mr Knowles, was probably less than 100 years old then. There were a number of sumps in the town, this particular one, besides being central, served the fish-market across the Square on the west corner of the old Hog-Market Lane, where there was another pump. Another pump in Conduit Street, near the Creek quay, was still used by fishermen in my earlier days. There was another pump in Tanner Street.

It was Edward's son, Harry, who continued the business and combined it with prominence in local politics. He was a member of Faversham Borough Council 1936-70: Mayor in 1949: an Alderman from 1961, and when on retirement he was made a freeman of the borough, he was only the eighth person to be so recognised since the Freedom was instituted in 1885. But the family individuality stood out, for even when chairman of the local Conservative Branch, he still stood, as always, for election as an Independent. Moreover, in 1961, as Alderman, he fell out with the local Conservatives, and although not needing to do so, put up for election as a Councillor. He was duly elected, and immediately resigned, thereby causing a by-election.

Edward's other son, Charlie, who lived in Jaffa House, Whitstable, and ran the business in that town, was a member of Whitstable Town Council, but was often frustrated by Standing Orders which cut down his contributions to debate. One evening he stormed out of a meeting, locking the door from the outside on the way, so that the august

Council was temporarily imprisoned in its own meeting place!

It was Charlie, also, who objected to the installation of traffic lights at the junction of Oxford Street and Canterbury Road, where a policeman and had often directed traffic, just down from Jaffa House. When they began to operate, he drove out in his car, waited till the signal turned red, and then proceeded to ignore them and drive slowly through. A policeman on the path to watch the working of the lights, diplomatically looked the other way when he saw Mr Knowles, who then tooted the car horn to call his attention, and waved enthusiastically as he went by. My brother John was driving behind in his own car - stopped at the lights, of course.

It was this member of the family, also, who at 7.30 one morning, went out in his carpet slippers, with his morning paper, to the yard behind Jaffa House where some of his staff awaited their daily orders, in days when the cost of living was just being calculated in points. He announced to them, *"Just listen to this, the cost of living has just gone up two points. It's going to cost more to live. That means, doesn't it, that I can't pay you so much"* . It was a huge joke, for they were a kindly and generous family, and was another way of expressing disapproval of these new-fangled ways of calculation and of doing things, like some of his father's advertisements.

Advertisements? Perhaps I should have said I was highlighting 'Publicity'. But we must end - there are so many adverts. Just after the last one I quoted in 1919, Edward is selling *"Large apples for stewing 2d per lb, five pounds for ninepence. And 'Faversham News' Free to Buyers of five pounds' also to buyers of five pounds of Green Victoria Plums for Stewing and Bottling 4d a lb."*

Later on, he addresses *"My dear Reader"*, on the live issue of the *"Open Market"*, thought to be *"some new thing"*. 'It is no new thing as far as Faversham is concerned. For nearly thirty years your old friend Knowles has discarded the old-fashioned idea of closed shutters and closed doors, and recognised the need of Open Market, and no profiteering' - a clever use of the fact that the Preston Street shop was completely open when in operation - no windows, no doors.
On another occasion he enumerates profits of landlords, farmers, growers, auctioneers, wholesalers, and the rest, and sums up, *"Buy of Knowles and save five of these profits - your old friend Knowles"*.

Yes, he was a friend. They all were. He distributed freely oranges and apples to children in Workhouse, schools, and at all the Church's Sunday Treats in the area. Many a year did we, from our early days, file out from the uproarious Christmas Treat of the 250 scholars at the St Mary's Road Baptist Sunday School, to receive, as we left, from the hand of Edward or his wife, standing inside the two entrances of the hall, a lovely orange, wrapped in those days, in tissue paper, and sometimes some nuts or an apple. So did all the many children in our numerous Sunday Schools.

"Knowles Greengrocer Faversham".

We shall never see their like again.

Surnames linked to The Knowles Family

Ackhurst
Arnold
Attwood
Badcock
Bertram
Butler
Cavell
Chalkraft
Clowes
Cornwell
Coster
Couchman
Cox
Dodd
Draper
Dunn
Dutton
Edell
Epps
Farmes
Field
French
Fuller
Gambier
Gardler
Hall
Hams
Harris
Honey
Horton
Hubbard
Hull
Hunt
Ince
Jackson
Jenkins
Johnson
Jones
Kelly
Kennett
Knight
Latham
Longley
Mansfield
Martin
McAnulty
McDermott
Miller
Mitchell
Moore
Newman
Nickels
O'Rielly
Pain
Pankhurst
Parker
Parton
Partridge
Paz
Phipps
Roche
Rogers
Ryan
Salmon
Sander
Saunders
Savine
Simpson
Sinclair
Skillen
Smeed
Smith
Stillwell
Stringer
Strouts
Tappenden
Thomas
Thompson
Tidy
Turner
Tutt
Waller
Webster
Wells
Wilbraham
Wildish
Wiles
Williams
Wilson
Woolf
Wright

Printed in Great Britain
by Amazon